The Enemy *of* Engagement

The Enemy of
Engagement

Put an End to Workplace Frustration—
and Get the Most from Your Employees

Mark Royal and Tom Agnew

∤AMACOM

American Management Association
New York • Atlanta • Brussels • Chicago • Mexico City • San Francisco
Shanghai • Tokyo • Toronto • Washington, D.C.

Bulk discounts available. For details visit:
www.amacombooks.org/go/specialsales
Or contact special sales:
Phone: 800-250-5308
E-mail: specialsls@amanet.org
View all the AMACOM titles at: www.amacombooks.org

This publication is designed to provide accurate and authoritative information in regard to the subject matter covered. It is sold with the understanding that the publisher is not engaged in rendering legal, accounting, or other professional service. If legal advice or other expert assistance is required, the services of a competent professional person should be sought.

Library of Congress Cataloging-in-Publication Data

Royal, Mark, 1967–
    The enemy of engagement : put an end to workplace frustration—and get the most from your employees / Mark Royal and Tom Agnew.
        p.   cm.
    Includes index.
    ISBN 978-0-8144-1795-9 (HC); ISBN 978-0-8144-3908-1 (PB);
    ISBN 978-0-8144-1796-6 (ebook)
    1. Employee motivation.   2. Job satisfaction.   3. Performance.
4. Organizational effectiveness.   5. Management.   I. Agnew, Thomas
George Arnold.   II. Title.

    HF5549.5.M63R69   2012
    658.3'14—dc23

                                                    2011017499

About AMA
American Management Association (www.amanet.org) is a world leader in talent development, advancing the skills of individuals to drive business success. Our mission is to support the goals of individuals and organizations through a complete range of products and services, including classroom and virtual seminars, webcasts, webinars, podcasts, conferences, corporate and government solutions, business books, and research. AMA's approach to improving performance combines experiential learning—learning through doing—with opportunities for ongoing professional growth at every step of one's career journey.

Printing number
10 9 8 7 6 5 4 3 2 1

Contents

Acknowledgments

FROM THE TIME we began this process seven years ago, we have benefited from our clients' desire to learn more about their organizations. We are grateful for their willingness to partner with us to explore the ideas presented in this book when few other organizations or consulting firms were focused on workplace frustration and employee enablement. While it would be impossible to acknowledge them all here, we offer special thanks to Karin Mayhew of Health Net, Inc., Gary Short of Kimberly-Clark, Rachel Levy of Daiichi Sankyo, and Steve Denault of COUNTRY Financial, who have been particularly generous in sharing with different audiences their experiences in monitoring and managing these issues.

Our colleagues within Hay Group Insight, Hay Group's employee research division, have also provided important input and guidance. We thank Will Werhane, our Global Managing Director, and members of our Global Management Team, including Ben Hubbard, Michele Goldberg, Mikito Ichikawa, and Andy Tunnard, for their support for our research program in general and this project specifically. The work of our Advanced Research Services group, Rebecca Masson, Juran Hulin, and Kerry-Ann

McKnight, was critical in developing, refining, and validating the research behind the ideas presented in this book.

Additionally, we would like to express our appreciation for the contributions of a number of other Hay Group colleagues: Tom McMullen, Rick Lash, and Brian Langham for providing thoughtful and helpful feedback on drafts of the manuscript; Stephen Welch for perspectives on employee engagement and employee enablement in the communications, media, and technology sector; Bibi Hahn, Timis Rallis, Katie Lemaire, Jean-Marc Laouchez, Brian Langham, and Andreas Raharso for perspectives on strategic performance management; Mitch Kent for connecting us with AMACOM and Louis Greenstein; and Nick Boulter, Mary Fontaine, and David Harkleroad for their sponsorship of this effort.

Louis Greenstein and Tina Waters deserve a special note of acknowledgment. Louis provided his talents to ensure that the narrative story of Bernette Financial was effectively written and that our technical chapters were clear and meaningful. And Tina provided invaluable insight into call center operations. We also want to recognize the contributions of the editorial staff at AMACOM, specifically Christina Parisi, Barry Richardson, and Erika Spelman.

On a personal level, we owe a debt of gratitude to our families. We thank our spouses, Terry Royal and Nicole Theriot, for their support throughout this project and for sharing our excitement about making our book idea a reality. Their friendly but candid feedback is reflected throughout the final product. Ellen and Jim Royal also helped us resolve some key questions about character names. We recognize that a "thank-you" to our families cannot adequately convey our appreciation. And that's why we dedicate this book, with love, to them.

The Enemy *of* Engagement

Introduction

WE INITIATED the research behind this book seven years ago in response to our experiences working with a number of organizations that were struggling to translate high levels of employee motivation into better individual, team, and organizational performance. A noteworthy example comes from an employee opinion survey we and our team at Hay Group conducted in 2004 for a new client in the pharmaceutical industry. While the results were highly favorable overall, and confirmed strong employee engagement throughout the organization, there were some troubling signals coming from the management layer immediately below the executive level. Given the importance of these individuals to the company for executing on current strategies and as future leaders of the business, we were asked to explore the situation further through a series of one-on-one interviews.

To a person, the managers we interviewed confirmed the high levels of motivation and commitment the survey results had indicated (*"I've never worked for a better company." "I'm excited about our future."*). Yet, positive statements about the company were typically coupled with a pause and a *"but . . ."*

What followed were concerns about the ability of these engaged managers to get things done in the organization because of issues involving objectives and priorities (*"Everything is urgent." "Make a decision and move on, instead of rehashing old arguments."*), interdependencies across the organization (*"Why does every decision have to go through twelve people?" "Everyone can't expect to touch everything as in the past."*), relationships with the parent organization overseas (*"Everything has to be pitched to the parent company. It's hard to secure resources for things that don't directly impact sales."*), and accountabilities for performance (*"We tend to manage around performance problems. It's very discouraging."*).

These managers were committed to the company, aligned with its goals, and anxious to contribute. But they were *frustrated* by barriers in the work environment confronting them and their teams. After identifying similar issues in many other organizations, we knew we were tapping into a significant, but often overlooked, threat to both employee engagement and individual and organizational success.

Managers are bombarded with messages about how important it is to motivate and inspire their people. Very little attention, however, has been given to how managers can most effectively translate employee motivation into optimal levels of performance. Unfortunately, the commitment and discretionary effort offered by engaged employees can be squandered if managers are not careful to position employees in roles that fully leverage their potential and to provide them with the workplace supports they need to carry out their responsibilities. In a real sense, workplace frustration is the enemy of engagement.

This book is targeted at anyone charged with directly managing the day-to-day activities of a group of employees. We'll be using an example from a fictional company to illustrate both the impact of frustration on employees and the approaches managers can take to address it. While Bernette Financial and the characters we'll meet may not exist, the organizational context is very real and is based on situations we have observed in many companies. We'll follow the Bernette story through the odd-numbered chapters in the book, while in the even-numbered chapters we will provide perspectives and recommendations for managers derived from Hay Group research.

In Chapters 1 and 2, we introduce the concept of workplace frustration. We explain both what it is (a highly engaged employee's inability to succeed in a role due to organizational barriers or the inability to bring the bulk of his or her talents, skills, and abilities to the job) and what it is not (demotivation, dissatisfaction). We highlight common responses to frustration exhibited by employees and the negative consequences these reactions often have for individuals and organizations. Finally, we explore why leaders in today's organizations are frequently poorly positioned to identify and respond to workplace frustration.

In Chapters 3 and 4, we differentiate employee engagement (motivating employees to succeed) from employee enablement (giving them the ability to perform effectively). We discuss engagement and enablement as distinct concepts that are influenced by different organizational factors and managerial behaviors. And we review research confirming that both are necessary for optimum performance; that is, high levels of engagement are not sustainable without enabling work conditions.

In Chapters 5 and 6, we call attention to the "tenure effect" commonly observed in organizations. Employee opinion trends consistently show that people are never as engaged as they are in their first year on the job—and that engagement levels tend to drop steadily with longer tenures. The common explanation is that expectations for jobs are not properly set in advance and, therefore, individuals become disillusioned as they begin to understand what their jobs actually entail. Organizations commonly respond by attempting to establish more appropriate expectations or to integrate employees into the organization and their roles more effectively (e.g., through realistic job previews or onboarding programs). However, in our view the true solution lies with employee enablement. As employees grow in experience in their roles, they begin to focus less on learning the ropes and more on achieving desired results. In the process, they are increasingly confronted with enablement constraints that limit their ability to get their jobs done effectively. Organizations need to understand that the key to keeping employees engaged over time is ensuring that they are well enabled.

With an understanding of frustration, its manifestations, and its implications, we focus in Chapters 7 and 8 on a systematic review of root causes. We explore in detail the primary determinants of employee enablement. And we drill down within these determinants to identify key aspects of the work environment that should be focus areas for managers in understanding current enablement levels within their teams.

After calling attention to work environment considerations enablement-focused managers need to monitor and address, in Chapters 9 and 10 we turn our attention to strategies for minimizing workplace frustration. We provide a self-assessment that features a series of questions managers can consider, individually or with their teams, in relation to each enablement determinant. We also offer best-practice recommendations for addressing opportunities for improvement that are identified.

While there is much managers can do on their own to position motivated employees to succeed, they clearly need support from senior leaders in creating a focus on, and accountability for, employee enablement throughout an organization. In Chapters 11 and 12, we discuss the role of managers as organizational change agents, giving a voice to frustrated employees and elevating awareness of enablement issues as essential to sustaining high levels of individual and team performance over time.

By the end of this book, you will understand what workplace frustration is, the negative consequences it has on individuals and organizations, how to diagnose it and its root causes within your team, and how to take effective action to promote higher levels of employee enablement and unleash the full potential of your people.

CHAPTER 1

There's Something Happening Here

It began with a text message from Lauren Duffy to her boss, Beth Charles. "We need to talk. Lunch today?" Beth studied the message on her cell phone and sighed. "We need to talk" seldom heralds good news.

Beth was at her desk in her small private office at Bernette-Online, the Internet division of the popular financial institution that opened its "brick and mortar" doors back in 1967 in suburban Denver, Colorado.

Bernette Financial was one of the first community banks to enter the online market. Named after its founders Bernard and Annette Ellsworth, Bernette got its start as a community bank, serving businesses and individuals with residential and commercial mortgages, small-business loans, checking and savings accounts, certificates of deposit, retirement accounts, savings clubs, and other financial products. Almost from the outset, the small bank with strong local roots became one of the region's most popular institutions. Bernie and his wife, Annette, appeared in the bank's television ads. The appeal was immediate: Bernie and Annette were fun-loving, homey types who'd grown up in Denver and raised their children there. They were real people. It came across in the ads as well as at the bank. Bernie was accessible, humorous, and—according to past and present employees—the best CEO anyone could ask for. Around him was a team of highly respected VPs, personable, competent, and hardworking. The bank's mission statement: "Our products improve our customers' lives."

It was Bernie and Annette's son, Howard, who had the vision to take Bernette Financial online. Back east, a few years out of graduate school, Howard had taken an interest in e-commerce. With technical help from one of his undergraduate friends from the University of Pennsylvania, the prototype for Bernette's Internet banking system was developed. After selling Bernie and a couple of the bank's officers on the potential for online banking, where customers could complete transactions at home or through ATM machines without ever having to step into a branch, Howard returned to Denver to direct the online enterprise. "Welcome to the future of our bank," Bernie had proclaimed.

The launch of BernetteOnline was a major event in the Rocky Mountain region and across the nation as well. It got a lot of good press, and Bernie Ellsworth enjoyed being in the limelight. The bank's cutting-edge technology, combined with its fun culture, its reputation for integrity, and its commitment to the community, put BernetteOnline front and center in newscasts, newspapers, and banking industry publications. *Fast Track* magazine did a big feature that included interviews with Bernie and Howard. Other banks may have been doing what Bernette was doing online, but not with the success, the confidence, or the promise of expanding in bigger and better directions.

"We need to talk." As vice president of call center operations, Beth was accustomed to a certain amount of employee turnover. This was, after all, a call center. And even though Bernette had dramatically lower turnover than most of its peers, some attrition was bound to occur. But Lauren? No, not Lauren, she hoped. "What else might she need to talk about?" Beth wondered to herself. A leave of absence? Could be. Her husband's mother was in the process of moving from an apartment in Albuquerque, New Mexico, to an assisted living facility. Perhaps Lauren needed a couple of weeks off to help with the transition. Or, since Lauren's stepson was taking his junior year of college abroad, maybe Lauren and her husband were planning to visit him in Amsterdam.

Over the past eight years, Lauren and Beth had become close friends as well as coworkers. On paper, Lauren, whose title was "workforce management specialist," reported to Beth. But for years, Beth had thought of Lauren as her secret weapon. While Beth was responsible for overall operations, Lauren was a gifted problem solver whose ability to forecast future needs, staff the call center appropriately, and ensure ongoing product training was widely respected at Bernette.

Beth attributed Lauren's skill to her earlier training in industrial design. In fact, Lauren came from a family that was well-known in design circles. Her father, Phil Brown, had led the research and development on the first electric toothbrush designed for the consumer market back in the 1960s. As a young girl, Lauren spent hundreds of hours in her dad's workshop—building inventions, reworking old plans, and learning the fine art of creative problem solving. "My dad is a designer," Lauren would joke, "and I got the talent from him. I guess you could call it 'designer genes.'"

Lauren earned her bachelor's degree in industrial design and began a career in the field. But soon after she had her children, she decided to get away from the deadline-driven R&D environment, and the sixty-plus-hour workweeks that came with the job, and work part-time until her children were in school. Responding to an ad for a call center job at Bernette, she made a huge impression during her initial interview. When the interviewer from HR mentioned that the call center used an Excel spreadsheet for forecasting shifts, Lauren began to think about a better solution, software that could do a better job forecasting because it could look at exceptions faster and more accurately than an individual can eyeball them on a spreadsheet. She mentioned her idea to the interviewer, who listened with interest. "Management Potential," she wrote on Lauren's résumé. Two days later, Lauren interviewed with Beth, who was the workforce management specialist at the time. She quickly offered Lauren the part-time call center job she sought, and she hoped to retain her as a full-time manager when her children got a bit older.

～

Bernie Ellsworth, the bank's founder, had recently announced that he was planning to retire. But Bernie's departure wasn't cause for concern. For years he had groomed Howard to take over as CEO. Everyone knew that Howard had the credentials: a Wharton MBA and twenty years of experience in financial services, including more than a decade at Bernette. The bank was doing well and had earned a coveted spot on *Business Today*'s "Best Places to Work" list in seven of the past ten years.

Everyone loved Bernie and Howard, but neither of them had the internal focus the bank needed at this stage. Bernie had always relied on strong personal relationships, both within the organization and with customers and the community, to operate and grow the business. Informal connections among people who had worked together for years and shared common understandings of how things were done had provided an adequate operating system when the bank was small. But Bernette had merged with a competitor, Green Tree Financial, in the past year, and this, coupled with several years of strong organic growth, had made operations considerably more complex. For his part, Howard was a visionary who had brought new thinking to the bank about products and services and the potential for Bernette in a changing financial services sector; his passion and focus centered on new markets and new products.

It was clear to Beth that the call center and other parts of the organization had been experiencing more operational issues over the past few years. Costs were increasing faster than revenues, sending the organization into cost-control mode. Right after the merger, the two banks' call centers were consolidated, but there were still two different customer relationship management (CRM) systems operating, and neither one could "talk" to the other. When Lauren submitted a postmerger proposal for new CRM software to integrate Green Tree's and Bernette's products, she was told she'd have to wait and that the call center reps would have to continue using outdated tools for the time being.

Lauren took her concern to Beth. "I understand that there are a lot of competing priorities right now," she said. "But my people can't do their jobs without resources. They love their work; I don't even have to tell you how committed they are. But we need to provide them with adequate tools and support." Lauren had a point.

The reps were taking all this in stride, even though their service levels were beginning to drop. They trusted that the issue would be addressed eventually.

Beth reread Lauren's message, checked her schedule, and texted back. "Sure. Noon?"

Her text message sent, Beth looked at her calendar to see what she needed to accomplish before her mystery lunch with Lauren. "Do something about Bob" was number one on her to-do list.

Bob Joseph was one of the nicest people she'd ever met. A five-year employee, Bob was bright and disciplined, kind and easy to get along with. He worked as a rep in the call center, specializing in escalations and high-level problem solving for customers. He had achieved this senior-rep position by virtue of his unshakable patience and his product knowledge. No one was better than Bob at gaining a complete understanding of new products. Because Bob was such a good writer, he worked mostly on e-mail responses, and only occasionally on the telephone.

Just one problem: Of all the reps in the call center, Bob was the slowest. His service levels were below everyone else's when it came to the number of e-mails resolved per hour. But he had the call center's highest level of customer satisfaction. Beth studied his six-month review and the action plan his supervisor Stacy had prescribed. The entire plan was designed to get Bob to work faster and resolve more customer issues per hour.

Bob had a second career as a fiction writer. His short stories appeared in magazines, and a couple of his plays had been produced at a small Denver theater. Interestingly, after attending the opening night of one of Bob's plays a few months ago, Beth got into a conversation with Bernette's director of marketing communications, Rich DeCurtis. "We love Bob," Beth told Rich. "He is slow and deliberate, but he gives the customers the best information. You should see his e-mails," she said.

Rich listened intently to Beth's description of Bob. It gave him an idea.

"What if he came over to marketing and worked as a technical writer?" Rich asked Beth. "We need someone to rewrite the entire customer service section of the website and draft templates of the most common customer service response e-mails." Presently, Rich said, there was no technical writer in the department. Everyone took turns working on the website, the e-mail templates, and the myriad other writing projects that came up. The result was a patchwork of communications in a variety of styles and voices, a mishmash of features and benefits. Bob could surely clean it all up. Plus, the department had ongoing needs for a writer with strong Bernette product knowledge to work on promotional e-mails, special offers, and customer education.

Beth studied Bob's last couple of reviews and concluded he was never going to pick up speed. But he had so many virtues—always on time, always willing to stay late or come in early, helpful at trainings, and a goodwill ambassador who made new reps feel right at home on their first day. Yet he was making no progress on his action plan. His service levels had not improved.

Beth wrote an e-mail to George Franken, the senior VP of marketing, asking for his help with some red tape that was preventing Bob's move from the call center. She spelled out in detail how if Bob were to move to marketing and take over all Web content and customer service e-mail templates, marketing would not have to hire an additional associate as planned. "Since we're all being asked to control costs," Beth wrote to George, "this arrangement would close a big hole in our communications strategy without your having to make any new marketing hires. We will need to hire someone at the call center to replace Bob Joseph," she wrote, "but that's a relatively minor expense, especially if you consider the value that Bob's writing skills would add to the bank. George, I've been working with Bob for five years. You won't find a more loyal and willing employee." *Moving Bob to marketing is a win-win,* Beth told herself as she clicked "send."

"*We need to talk.*" Beth shuddered. "That's how insecure men break up with their girlfriends."

During the five-minute drive to the restaurant, Lauren and Beth didn't actually talk much. And what they did cover was minor. Lauren drove while Beth checked her Blackberry. There was a parking space right in front of their favorite Italian restaurant. Once inside, they both ordered iced teas. In an awkward silence they waited for their drinks and a breadbasket. When the iced teas arrived, they each took a sip, then faced each other, still in silence.

Finally, Beth made the first inroad. "What do you want to talk about?" she asked.

Lauren put down her glass and reached over for a piece of bread. She studied the grain on the bread, lines etched in crust. She'd rehearsed what she was about to say, but she was still finding it difficult. *Out with it!* she told herself.

"I'm concerned," she began, "that the growth at Bernette is going to undermine the culture, which everyone in the call center will tell you is the best thing about working there."

"I hear you," said Beth warily. She knew Lauren well enough to know that she was holding something back. "But drop the other shoe," she told her friend.

Lauren took a deep breath and announced, "I'm . . . looking around."

Beth looked up from her menu, her eyes wide. "The company isn't going to be as much fun as it used to be, so you're planning to leave?"

Lauren shook her head. "It's not just the fun. Remember, I'm a forecaster and I am accustomed to thinking three or four steps ahead. Right now, people are happy. They still love working at Bernette. But with service levels dropping and a new emphasis on saving money without investing in new tools for the reps, I don't think morale will remain high, and I'm afraid that might reflect poorly on me."

Beth knew what Lauren was talking about. A lot had changed at Bernette over the past few years. The informal communication approach Bernette had relied on in the past was breaking down in the larger organization, and that hurt everyone. Twice in the past four months, the legal department had scheduled mandatory training for call center reps to take place over a three-day period. But no one in the call center received this information until it was too late. Instead of having two or three weeks to schedule shift changes and authorize overtime, Lauren had just two days to schedule around the training. With no overtime to offer and less than forty-eight hours' notice, she just couldn't get enough staff in to make up for those who were off-site for the training. Both times the results were disastrous: skeleton crews handling twice the normal volume of calls, service levels plummeting, dozens of escalations, and hundreds of complaints.

And worse yet: Three weeks earlier, Ray Pough, the bank's highly respected and long-serving COO, had quit his job for reasons that were still unclear. That was a jolt. Ray had been with Bernette for his entire twenty-five-year career; he was a friend of the Ellsworth family. His departure stung everyone.

"You know," Lauren told Beth, "what we have is unique. You go down to that call center, walk up to any rep and ask them why we do what we do, you know what you will hear? 'We're here to help people save money and improve their lives. We're here to help people afford the homes they want. We're here to help businesses grow and prosper. We're here for the community.'

"That's our brand," said Lauren. "And we've worked hard to build it. This organization shows a tremendous amount of integrity to the call center representatives, which is why they love Bernette. It's why, unlike their peers at nearly every other call center around, they aren't cynical. It's why they stay loyal. They bought the T-shirt, Beth, and wear it proudly. But now things are changing. I can feel it. Howard's a great guy. He's visionary; he gets our strategy. But I'm concerned about what happens to the call center as the bank grows. It's one thing to be engaged and loyal. But if you can't accomplish what you're supposed to, being engaged in the work just isn't enough."

The waitress came to take their orders—vegetarian ravioli for Beth, Italian wedding soup and Caesar salad for Lauren. After eating in silence for a minute, Beth put down her fork, wiped her lips with her napkin, cleared her throat, and addressed Lauren. "Are you giving your notice?"

Lauren gritted her teeth. "No."

"Well, that's a relief," said Beth.

"Not yet, anyway," added Lauren. She could see the hurt on Beth's face.

Beth sipped from her glass of water and took a couple bites of a breadstick. "Losing you would be worse for call center morale than losing Ray Pough last month," she said. "What do you think you'd be looking for if you decide to leave?"

Lauren thought for a moment. "I like the feeling of accomplishment. You know? You set out to do something. You have a goal in mind. I like when I accomplish the goal. It makes me feel good. So I'd look for a job where I would get that feeling, where I could help to improve things, not watch something great slip away and not be able to help."

The call center was in desperate need of new CRM tools. The tools Beth wanted would cut each call by a minute or two because the new technology would put products and solutions right on the rep's monitor, instead of requiring the rep to key in a code. Last year at the Call Center Expo both Beth and Lauren had tried the tool—and it blew them away. They couldn't wait to write the proposal, develop a working prototype, and get the reps trained on it. Lauren created a forecast that showed how the new tool would handle calls so much faster that Bernette would be able to scale back on its fourth-quarter hiring, all the while improving service levels even as call volume grew! Yet the purchase wasn't approved. Shortly after that, the bank merger went through, capital improvements were put on hold indefinitely, and Ray Pough resigned.

Beth blew on a forkful of ravioli and nibbled at the shell. "Okay," she said, "right now getting resources is a challenge, and getting information so we can schedule our people—that's a challenge too. But Howard's heart is in the right place, and he loves this bank."

After a brief pause, Beth continued. "So, have you interviewed?"

Lauren sipped her iced tea. "I sent out a couple résumés. That's as far as I've gotten."

Beth looked Lauren in the eye. "Is this a definite thing? Or just a possibility, you know, if things don't get better?"

"You know me," said Lauren. "I don't make rash moves. I am not making any decisions right now except that I will get some résumés out there, and I'll interview anywhere that calls. And you should know, it's not like I'm ready for a career change. My daughters are too young for me to spend so much time at work." She took a couple more spoonfuls of her soup, then picked up a fork and dabbed at her salad.

Both women knew that things at Bernette were changing. Both had recently become aware that Stacy Robbins, the daytime shift supervisor, was burning out. And why wouldn't she? "Look at it from Stacy's point of view," said Lauren. "She's the one who has to face the sixty reps who arrive for a shift only to learn that the other sixty were pulled out for an off-site. And she's the one who is most affected by having two CRM systems. We have to integrate those systems. No one can keep pace. If this keeps up, you know as well as I do that we'll be losing reps like nobody's business."

Beth put down her knife and fork. She looked at Lauren. She respected her—as a friend and as a colleague. She didn't want to lose her. She didn't want to lose Stacy either. And she didn't want to lose call center reps, not at the rate that other organizations lost them. Bernette's call center had the lowest turnover rate in the industry. But would it continue?

"Of course I can't stop you from interviewing, from finding a new job, or from turning in your resignation. I understand what you are telling me. Now, will you give me a chance to address what's going on here?"

Lauren nodded. She had sent out only two résumés, and no one from those employers had called her yet. In truth, she was ambivalent about leaving. There was so much to like about Bernette. It was a great institution founded by great people. Perhaps it was simply experiencing growing pains. It was a good place to work. But these days, Lauren and employees like her, while feeling engaged, loyal, and ready to work, were finding themselves unable to achieve their goals. Lauren, because of her nature, couldn't help being concerned about the long-term prospects.

"Sure," she told Beth. "If you can figure out what's going on around here, and if you can turn it around so that it will continue to be a great place to work, you can count on me to stick around."

CHAPTER 2

Frustration:
The Silent Killer

THE BERNETTE FINANCIAL call center culture is the envy of the industry. Turnover is low. Nearly every employee believes in the mission: They're helping people buy homes, helping businesses serve their communities, and helping families achieve their dreams. Customer surveys invariably show that Bernette customers are overall "very satisfied" with the help they get when they call or e-mail. Questions get answered. Problems get resolved. Customer service representatives are viewed as helpful, knowledgeable, and friendly.

By and large, Bernette call center employees are engaged and committed to the success of the organization. But is engagement enough? Let's look at the situations faced by the employees we've met so far.

Lauren made her mark on the call center by figuring out a better way to forecast scheduling needs. She is self-motivated to be efficient and effective. Solving a vexing problem is its own reward for her. She wants to work in a challenging environment that allows her to continue to be successful. If her current employer doesn't offer one, she is confident that another employer will.

Lauren's boss, Beth, recently witnessed the departure of a long-term, highly valued executive at the bank. And she knows she might lose another valuable employee, Lauren, unless she can open up the flow of information and get the resources that Lauren and her direct reports need so that they can continue to do their jobs well. Beth is also grappling with the situation faced by Bob, the customer service rep with the highest customer satisfaction ratings but the slowest completion rate. She is having trouble getting approval to transfer Bob to the marketing department, where he'll be a better fit and continue to make a valuable contribution to Bernette.

Stacy is a long-term Bernette employee who is struggling with scheduling issues. She isn't getting the information she needs from Lauren so that she can schedule reps for optimum results.

And Bob is in a job that doesn't make the best use of his capabilities.

All these employees are motivated and want to succeed. They all have a high regard for the bank's leaders and believe in the bank's mission. They want to "do more with less" just as they are being asked to do. But due to constraints in the work environment, they can't, and that has them feeling *frustrated*.

This isn't a case of temperamental, indifferent, or intellectually challenged management. Bernette has a well-earned reputation for being a great place to work. Its executives are known as competent and caring individuals. But the organization, like many today, is undergoing change. It's growing, organically and through acquisition, and its senior leaders are focused on managing expenditures at a time when the bank's costs are increasing faster than its revenues. As popular as they are with call center employees, the bank's senior executives might not sense the frustration of the reps who can't do their jobs without the right tools, or of the supervisors who can't manage the call center as effectively as they once did.

The irony here is that the more loyal and engaged employees are, the deeper their frustration will run in the face of obstacles. Simply put, they are frustrated *because* they care.

This book is focused on employees who are engaged, motivated, and loyal—who aren't ready to give up—but who are experiencing frustration on the job.

Frustration: Fulfillment Denied

Frustration is a daily occurrence that affects almost everyone: the man who can't get to work because the bus drivers are on strike or the woman craving her morning cup of coffee but whose husband forgot to pick up milk at the grocery store.

Frustration is a common emotional response to opposition, when the human will seeks a certain fulfillment but cannot get what it wants. Frustrated people have a desired goal or objective in mind. They want to achieve something, but they are thwarted in their efforts. In general, the greater the desire and the obstruction, the bigger the sense of frustration. To individuals experiencing frustration, the emotion is usually attributed to external factors that are beyond their control. *It's not me, it's the striking bus drivers! If my husband had only remembered to pick up milk, I wouldn't be drinking black coffee!* An individual suffering from frustration will often feel powerless to change the situation.

Broadly speaking, people react either positively or negatively to frustration. Problem solving is a positive reaction to frustration. The person who is frustrated takes steps to remove the impediment instead of letting it overcome her. *I'll catch a cab instead of taking the bus. I'll pick up a decent cup of coffee at a coffee shop on the way to work.*

Unfortunately, not all responses to frustration are so constructive. Anger is one common negative reaction. It can take the form of verbal or even physical abuse, or some other violent reaction. Withdrawal is another common negative reaction to frustration. When faced with frustration, some people simply give up. This may take the form of either physically removing oneself from the frustrating situation or psychologically or emotionally detaching.

Frustration in the Workforce

When thinking about frustration as it plays out in the workplace, it is important to consider not only what it is, but also what it isn't. Commonplace notions of frustration call to mind individuals who frequently complain about things—the lack of available parking spaces, a nagging deadline, or a thermostat never set at the right temperature, for example. Certainly the little inconveniences of daily work life can be challenging and agitating. However, frustration in the workplace as we define it is a distinctly different phenomenon. In an organizational context, frustration is not as simple as failing to get something you want. Rather, it involves the inability to succeed in your role due to organizational barriers or the inability to bring the bulk of your individual talents, skills, and abilities to your job.

It is also important to understand the distinction between frustration, demotivation, and dissatisfaction. By definition frustrated employees are engaged and motivated; indeed, that state is a necessary precursor to the condition.

Frustration is created for those employees who are thwarted in their attempts to be successful despite their deep feelings of commitment and engagement. In other words, frustration is brought on by a belief in the organization and a desire to help it to be successful! Demotivated and disengaged employees simply don't care enough about organizational success to become deeply frustrated when they are not able to contribute to the success of the organization at an optimal level. They can shrug it off.

Frustration is also not dissatisfaction. Most frustrated employees do not walk around frowning and feeling negatively about the organization. In fact, frustrated employees, while perhaps dissatisfied with certain aspects of their work, are commonly satisfied with the organization as a whole. They usually don't complain. And that can make frustration difficult to identify.

But make no mistake: Frustration in the workplace is a silent killer. Frustrated employees are unlikely to persist over the long term in such a state. Where strong motivation to succeed is not paired with similar levels of support in the work environment, positive or negative reactions can be expected, just as with personal frustration. Former Ohio State University football coach Woody Hayes used to say that "there are three things that can happen when you pass, and two of them ain't good." Unfortunately, the same is true of the three responses to workplace frustration:

1. *A breakthrough.* Some engaged but frustrated employees may certainly, through force of effort, find ways to overcome

the barriers presented by low levels of support and upgrade their work arrangements to match their motivational levels. These employees are successful in using positive "problem-solving" approaches to dealing with their frustration.

2. *A breakdown.* Some employees, weary of beating their heads against a wall, may simply decide that giving their best effort is not worth their time; they'll simply stop trying.

3. *A clean break.* Still other frustrated employees can be expected to vote with their feet and leave in search of greener pastures where their strong motivation to succeed can be matched with more supportive working conditions, leading to an unfortunate brain drain of an organization's best and brightest talent.

Below is a verbatim comment from a frustrated employee, drawn from a recent employee opinion survey conducted for a Hay Group client:

> I need support, and my manager and his boss are not doing their best to provide it. I am inundated with work, and I end up staying here late each night. I root for the company and I think we are one of the good guys in the industry. I like my job despite this situation and I think things will change for the better eventually. But waiting for that time to come is very challenging. I'm almost ready to throw in the towel.

This comment reflects something that is common in many organizations. The individual is committed to the company and to his own job. He is anxious to make a positive contribution. But the lack of support from the organization and its leadership makes success hard to achieve. For the moment, this individual is still committed. He hasn't yet withdrawn. But there are ominous signs of potential disengagement and/or turnover.

No Complaints

Of particular importance to organizations is the fact that the frustrated employees who choose the *clean break* option are likely to be top performers or potential high performers. Why are they more likely to leave? First, because they *can*. They are particularly likely to have strong alternative career options available to them. They are, after all, among the most desirable individuals in the workforce. Second, highly capable employees who linger in an environment that does not allow them to be optimally productive are underleveraging their skills and suboptimizing the outcomes of their work. In other words, by staying in a nonsupportive work environment, they risk undermining their own opportunities for career advancement and increased compensation. Finally, as a matter of identity, achievement-oriented people may suffer from "cognitive dissonance," a psychologist's term for the feeling of discomfort that accompanies holding two or more contradictory ideas in one's head at the same time. If your restricted performance is at odds with your self-image as a high achiever, the conflict between your identity and your outputs may cause high levels of anxiety.

Hay Group research indicates that in organizations today, frustrated employees commonly represent 20 percent or more of the total workforce. But if there are so many truly frustrated employees out there, and the consequences are so significant, why aren't companies focused on actively addressing and managing this issue?

Unfortunately, most organizations are poorly positioned to recognize and respond to the concerns of frustrated employees. We have identified three basic reasons why this is the case. Either an organization

- ► Isn't asking them,
- ► Can't hear them, or
- ► Doesn't want to know.

Insofar as employee opinion surveys and other employee feedback programs have traditionally focused on employee satisfaction, commitment, and engagement, findings often fail to highlight issues related to the supportiveness of work environments.

Frustrated employees are also unlikely to voice their concerns in other ways. As they are typically highly committed to their employers and their jobs, many are disinclined to complain about their situations. They don't want to make waves. And those who do may be unlikely to press the point if their work arrangements are seen as unlikely to change.

But even if employee frustration is communicated to managers in one form or another, the messages do not always fall on receptive ears. While a lack of motivation can be viewed as a problem with the employee, a lack of support points the finger back at the organization. And addressing concerns about support for employee success may in some cases involve more fundamental changes to work arrangements than organizations are willing to tackle. Not all organizations want to face such hard truths. Many managers would rather identify a specific employee issue and tackle it than acknowledge the problem as having more systemic causes.

Frustration: A Global Issue

Beth, Lauren, Stacy, and the other Bernette employees we've met work in a U.S. financial services company call center. But the problem of frustration in the workplace is not unique to this setting. Far from it.

Hay Group research has confirmed that issues of frustration and a lack of organizational support for performance are not restricted to any particular job level, function, industry, or geography. As Figure 2.1 illustrates, looking across a number of major industry sectors, between 32 and 48 percent of employees report work conditions that do not allow them to be as productive as they could be.[1] It is this lack of organizational

Figure 2.1. Cross-industry concerns about supportiveness of work environment.

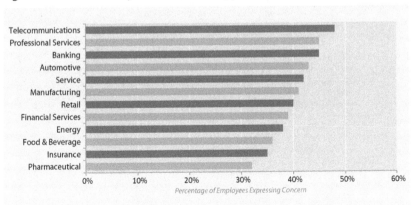

---

1. Based on Hay Group's employee opinion database, made up of responses from more than 4 million employees worldwide.

support that will produce frustration for the motivated and engaged employee.

Likewise, Figure 2.2 shows that frustration is also a global issue. Focusing on trends across forty-one countries around the world, we find consistent concerns expressed by employees regarding workplace supports for productivity. Not only is the

Figure 2.2. Cross-national concerns about supportiveness of work environment.

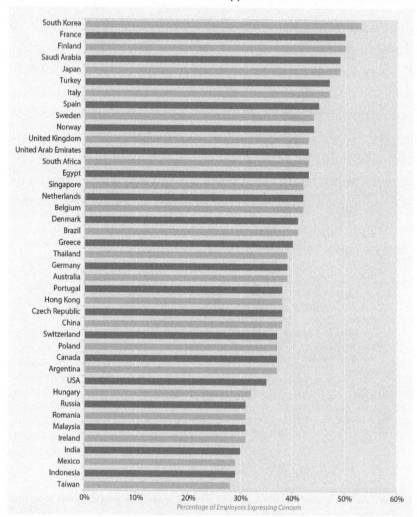

issue not limited to the United States, but these concerns are far more pronounced in many other countries.

Until organizations recognize and address workplace frustration, valuable resources will continue to be wasted. The irony is that frustrated workers want to contribute more than they currently can. They want to give their discretionary effort, but they are being held back by the very organizations that are asking them to do more.

CHAPTER 3

Workplace Frustration Spreads at Bernette

LONG BEFORE her current work frustrations had her thinking about looking for a new job, Lauren had begun to believe that call center work was actually a real career option for her, not just something she would do until her younger children were grown. Over the years, she came to realize that a call center is an organization's front line. And when that organization is in the business of helping people—when it serves the community—then the call center workers are helping to do good.

Sometimes, Bernette felt like a mission to Lauren. Lately, however, it had begun to feel a little like *Mission: Impossible*. Try as she might, Lauren was having trouble achieving her goals.

Back when Lauren was in college, if you had told her that she would end up working in a bank's call center, she'd have laughed it off. If you had told her that she would actually *like* the call center job and enjoy the challenges, then she'd have told you that you were crazy. In fact, when she ran into college friends and told them what she was doing, the reaction was often surprise. She'd been at the top of her class. She could have done anything she wanted. *But work at a call center?* Her old friends found that hard to grasp.

Sometimes Lauren would explain to the skeptics that she didn't work as a call center rep anymore, but that she analyzed call volume, maintained service levels, produced hiring forecasts, and scheduled shifts. "It involves a lot of design and planning," she'd say. But she could see her friends' eyes glaze over. "It may sound strange, I know. I liked being a customer service rep and helping customers. It was very rewarding. And now I'm really engaged in making the center run on time and as efficiently as possible. There are a lot of moving parts, and I enjoy the challenge."

Lauren looked up to her father more than anyone else she knew. Phil Brown was legendary in the world of consumer product design. An admitted "workaholic" during his long career, Phil regularly put in twelve-hour days only to return to his home workshop to puzzle, problem-solve, plan, and build. Lauren's favorite childhood memories were of helping her dad in his workshop, fetching tools, answering his "thinking out loud" questions, making careful notes of experiment after experiment that, while not always successful, usually helped Phil get a little closer to solving whatever problem confronted him.

"If you want a rewarding career," he told his children when they were growing up, "choose something that will allow you to solve problems and figure out how to help people. That will give you the best sense of satisfaction. You'll know you've found the right job if you work for a while, look up at the clock, and can't believe how much time went by."

Even in his retirement, Phil spent many happy hours tinkering in his workshop. He didn't need the money. He simply loved the work. Sometimes he worked for former clients on a consulting basis. Other times he worked for himself, designing improvements to his sailboat or building a new water ski prototype (to be field-tested by his grandchildren).

When Lauren got home from work on the day of her "we need to talk" lunch with Beth, she called her father on the telephone.

"Dad, things are changing at the bank," she told him. "Remember when I told you about the big merger? That was almost a year ago, and we're still using the old CRM system. All this time and there hasn't been an integration. They tell me it's a 'phase three' thing, but I don't know what that means or when phase three is going to launch."

"Sounds like you're burning out," said Phil.

Lauren thought about that for a moment. "It's not burnout," she said. "I'm never bored at work. I'm totally committed, and I still like the people I work for. They're great, but I think they're stretched too thin, and it's beginning to prevent me from being as effective as I used to be. That's what's really bugging me."

As the center's workforce-management specialist, Lauren had to assess the bank's needs and forecast a work schedule so that there would be enough reps on duty twenty-four/seven. Lately, though, when new products were launched, no one told her about new promotions, TV and radio ads, or anything else that drives call center volume. "It's no one in particular's fault," she explained to her father. "It's just that with all this growth, as often as not important information slips through the cracks and I don't get what I need in time to act on it."

Back when Bernette was smaller, Lauren would hear about new products or new marketing promotions informally, in casual exchanges with others at work. Based on what she heard, she would make a forecast for scheduling or hiring.

"In the old days," she told her father, "everyone knew what was happening. There were always conversations. 'There's a new tax regulation? I'm going to need to schedule some training sessions.' But now we're a lot bigger. We need more formalized communication systems, and we don't have them."

Phil listened on the other end of the phone. He felt bad for his daughter. He, more than anyone else, knew what she was capable of. "What happens when you can't schedule properly and you don't have enough people on a shift?" he asked.

Lauren sighed. "What happens is that service levels take a dip and customers complain. But how can I manage our staffing levels when I don't hear what the needs are in the first place? It's just incredibly frustrating."

She didn't tell her father about the recent conversation that her boss, Beth, had had with *her* new boss, Angela Lohan, the bank's senior vice president of operations. Angela was relatively new at Bernette, a Green Tree executive from marketing who moved over to the operations side after the merger. When Angela told Beth to do more with less, Beth responded, "That is exactly what we're trying to do, but I'm going to need a little help in order to make that happen!"

Beth realized that she sounded more defensive than she'd intended, because she thought Angela looked slightly irritated.

"I'm sorry," said Beth. "I didn't mean to—"

Angela cut her off. "I'm going to be blunt," she said. "It's crunch time. Every department is up against it. We're in this together. We're all on the same team."

Beth was stung. "I'm not sure you understand," she said. "I do know we're all on the same team, and I really don't mean to sound like I'm complaining." She felt her throat tighten and her shoulders tense up. "We're spending too much money on overtime," she told Angela. "If Lauren can get the resources she needs, we're going to see big savings in no time." Beth didn't mention to Angela that she and Lauren were putting in more hours than ever, trying to forecast staffing needs based on limited information. After all, she thought, that problem was only temporary. If it required a little sacrifice on her part, she was willing to make it, as long as it wasn't for too long. And she knew she could count on Lauren to be a good soldier. At least she *hoped* she could.

In Angela's office, however, Beth could see that the discussion was not going well. Angela just wasn't listening, and Beth wasn't about to go over her boss's head. It's not that the senior team members were bad people or that they weren't smart. It was just that their focus had shifted to external growth as they looked to lock up the Rocky Mountain region and gain market share nationally through the online division.

Still, it felt to Beth as though the call center was being neglected. All she wanted was to get back on the senior team's radar.

But everything Beth said seemed to make Angela bristle. "This isn't a complaint," Beth repeated, keeping her voice even, trying not to sound emotional. "Since we haven't integrated the two banks' CRM systems yet, I have reps who have to leave their seats every three or four calls to find other reps with the other CRM so they can answer customers' questions."

Angela raised an eyebrow. Beth finally had her attention. She continued. "Bernette's CRM system has only Bernette products on it. And the Green Tree CRM system has only Green Tree products. The banks are integrated, but the software that helps our reps talk about our products isn't. If you think about how long it takes a rep to find information that isn't available on his or her computer, and you multiply that by the number of reps and the number of calls, you can see that we just can't maintain service levels." Downstairs in the call center, reps were feeling frazzled, putting customers on hold—wreaking havoc on service levels—while they tracked down the information required to answer questions.

Angela folded her arms across her chest. "This is something we will be getting to, but it's not going to happen right now. I understand Lauren's concerns, and yours as well. But with all due respect, it doesn't help your case when I come in to work every morning and see three call center employees standing around talking in front of the building."

Beth couldn't believe her ears. Didn't Angela know what call center work was like? In a word, stressful! Didn't Angela know that formulas were used to determine how long callers will be waiting in a queue before a rep takes their calls, or that even bathroom breaks were scheduled? Didn't she realize that calls were monitored?

Beth measured her words carefully. "Angela," she began. "Every break is scheduled. Every rep puts in forty hours per week. Every minute they spend here is logged. All overtime is documented. Lauren can show you everything on paper."

"Not necessary," said Angela. "And I apologize, too. I didn't mean to cast aspersions on your staff. I know we have a world-class call center, and I'm aware of what you've done to keep attrition low. You and Lauren are fantastic, and so are your people. I know that the folks down there do good work. But for now, we'll just have to get them to hunker down and put in more of an effort."

The conversation was over. Beth thanked Angela and made her way out of the executive suite.

Beth decided that she would report this conversation to

Lauren, and after that she would not bring up any of these issues again. If management wanted her to do more with less, she would try her best. Clearly, everyone was in the same boat: overworked and stressed out. Her department needed good information and the right resources so that they *could* do more with less. She wanted the same thing senior management wanted. But, she realized, her hands were tied.

She promised herself: no complaints; nose to the grindstone; get the job done as best she could. If the call center lacked the resources, she would try not to sweat it. And if the new "do more with less" mantra were to have a negative impact on the incredibly high retention rate that the call center had enjoyed for years, well, so be it.

All Beth could do was hope that the extra hours she was putting in at night wouldn't last too long, because family time was important to her. And she knew that Lauren was experiencing the same feelings.

Beth would wait for "phase three," and she'd advise Lauren to do the same. If the changes didn't happen, well, she wasn't even going to think about that yet.

~~

The frustration weighed on Lauren too. The Sunday after hearing from Beth about her unsuccessful talk with Angela, Lauren's husband told her she seemed out of sorts on the way home from a brunch with friends. "Why so stressed? Everything okay?" he asked. "You were there at brunch, but you hardly seemed present."

It was then that Lauren decided to take a look at the job market. When they got home, she looked at the Sunday classifieds and registered with a couple of Internet job search sites.

She would tell Beth, she decided, because Beth was not just her boss, but her friend as well.

Lauren recalled her interview at Bernette all those years ago. It was actually during her second interview, with the call center VP who preceded Beth, that Lauren had the idea for what eventually turned into "CritSched," or Critical Scheduling. "The more information call center employees provide us about their personal schedules and the more they tell us about when they want overtime, the faster and more accurately we can schedule overtime when we need it," she said. Her interviewer was impressed that Lauren had used the word "we" instead of "you," and she was especially impressed at how quick Lauren was on her feet—learning about call center operations, asking smart questions, getting some clarification, and offering a potential solution. The interviewer knew that Lauren would never be happy as just a rep, but that the call center could be a good place for her to start. Once Lauren really understood how the operation worked she could be a great asset.

On that decisive Sunday night, Lauren poured herself a cup of coffee, booted up her personal computer, and found her old résumé stored there. She opened the document. It needed a major revision. She'd have to add her accomplishments at Bernette, and there were many. She recalled the commendations and congratulatory letters she'd received over the years, for being an effective manager; for saving money on scheduling, hiring, and training; and for her positive attitude and ingenuity.

Because at a call center everything is measured, it's easy to see a manager's metrics. After launching CritSched, Bernette found that its hiring and training costs were down by 5 percent.

Operations in the call center were more efficient than ever! For one thing, the reps on overtime were the reps who wanted overtime, so they tended to be more motivated during their shifts. With CritSched, call center operations improved on every front. Call times got shorter, customer satisfaction levels grew, and turnover shrunk.

"How much longer can I settle for middling?" she asked herself as she reviewed her old résumé. Lauren wasn't looking for a promotion, and she didn't even need to be recognized for her efforts. For her, doing a great job was its own reward. But lately, due to changes at the bank, she wasn't able to deliver what she knew she was capable of. Like most achievers, Lauren set high standards for herself. It was ironic, she thought, that she was being asked to deliver more while at the same time she was being held back from doing exactly that!

So Lauren began her job search. She'd been away from industrial design a long time, and she had found work she loved. Besides, her younger children were still in school, and industrial designers worked such long hours. So she decided to apply for management jobs at other call centers. If she were asked during an interview why she was planning to leave her current job, she'd tell them the truth: that she's frustrated because she lacks the resources she needs to be highly effective.

She didn't want to make her wanting to leave Bernette sound like sour grapes. She genuinely liked the individuals on the senior team. Angela was a nice person, even if her new role was stressing her out. And Bernie and Howard were both brilliant and funny. Unfortunately, after hearing about Beth's talk with Angela, Lauren had begun to wonder whether the little community bank that was founded to help improve people's lives would ever again be the kind of environment where someone like her could stretch her wings, work with a real sense of purpose, and be the best that she could be.

Lauren also thought about Stacy Robbins, the shift supervisor who reported to her. She, too, was feeling frustrated, though she wasn't the sort of person to complain. Stacy had actually been working at Bernette longer than anyone else in the call center. She had started part-time as a teller in a branch when she was still in high school. When BernetteOnline started up, she came over from banking operations and was promoted to supervisor within a year. And Lauren couldn't think of anyone better suited to the job. Stacy was the quintessential people person—always interested in others, always asking great questions, and able to make people feel not only comfortable, but also special when they were around her.

Stacy used to be great for the bank's morale. But lately, she had begun to change. One source of frustration involved Bob, who wrote well, had a great personality, and could handle the most difficult customers, but was ridiculously slow at responding to customers via e-mail. Supposedly, Lauren and Beth were working on a plan to transfer Bob to marketing, where he would work on the bank's website.

Now, despite Lauren's and Beth's assurances, Bob was about to endure yet another semiannual review where he knew he'd be told he was doing a great job on everything except his speed, and could he please try to work faster.

"I try to keep a positive attitude all the time," Bob told one of his coworkers. "I'm lucky to have this job. It's close to home, the hours are flexible, and I can work night shifts when I need to be home with my kids. Plus, it's fun. It's cool to help people with their financial needs. I like it when I e-mail customers answers to their questions and they write back to thank me. It's a great feeling. Out of all the reps here, I have the best record of solving problems in just one e-mail. I'm going to move up to marketing soon to help the bank do a better job communicating with customers."

Unfortunately, Stacy got some bad news right before Bob's review. It came in an e-mail from Lauren. It turned out that according to a new bank policy carried over from Green Tree, no employee on a performance improvement plan could be promoted. Only after the action plan was complete, and the required improvements made, could the promotion happen.

After reading the e-mail, Stacy walked straight to Lauren's office. "This is ridiculous," she said, slapping Bob's action plan down on her boss's desk. "It's a catch-22! A move to marketing will solve Bob's performance issues, but he isn't allowed to make the move until his performance issues are resolved! Lauren, the whole point of moving Bob is so that he can do what he does best. Everyone knows the move will be good for the bank, for the entire call center, for all our customers, and Bob isn't even slated for a very big raise in the new job."

Lauren shrugged. "I'm so sorry. I know how crazy it sounds, but that's the policy. I know Beth wants it to happen, but I don't think there's much she can do about it right now."

Stacy shook her head. "What am I supposed to tell Bob? I already told him about the promotion. It's a 'no-brainer.' Bob's been anticipating this move. He's been telling everyone about it; he's so proud. This is going to disappoint him."

"I hear you," said Lauren. "For now, Bob will have to wait. And in the meantime, keep working with him to get him up to speed. And once he *is*, we can put in for the promotion and no one should have a problem with it."

Stacy was adamant. "He's been here for years and he has

not improved his speed since he was six months into the job. He writes slowly. We've discussed this many times. He tries, but he can't. 'Slow and deliberate,' he tells me. That's how he was trained. He's a published author and his writing style is so clear that he has the highest satisfaction rating of anyone on e-mail. We're lucky to have him, but he could be doing so much more."

Lauren promised to bring the concern to Beth. "Sit tight," she told Stacy. "Just tell Bob we need to push his review back a couple weeks. Give Beth a chance to run this by HR again."

A few days later, Stacy gave Bob the news that his review was being pushed back while Beth worked with HR to make his promotion go through. He took it well, but Stacy could see the disappointment in his eyes. "I'm stuck in second gear," he mused to Stacy. "I want to shift into third and go faster, but I guess I just wasn't built that way."

The idea for Bob's shift to marketing was well received by his call center colleagues, who saw it as a good move for both Bob and the organization. And now it looked as though it was getting scrapped, not for any reason that made sense, but to comply with a leftover policy from a bank that had never been as successful at customer service as Bernette was. This infuriated Stacy, though she did her best to show a good face when she discussed it with Bob. "I can wait for a couple of months," Bob told her. "I'm willing to work with you and Lauren and Beth to try to get me upstairs where I'll be of more use."

Even as he spoke those words, Bob could feel his motivation begin to slip. What if they didn't promote him? he wondered. Would they keep him around? He would try again to pick up his speed, he decided. If he could do that, the promotion would definitely happen.

But what if he couldn't? Bob weighed his options. He could search for a new job, one in a marketing department where he could do the kind of technical writing he did best. He was afraid that if he couldn't get any faster he'd lose his current job at Bernette, and he knew it's always best to search for work when you have a job, not when you're unemployed and desperate. Besides, there was so much to like about Bernette. He didn't want to work anywhere else.

Stacy knew Bob pretty well. She could tell he was anxious. "Just give Beth and Lauren a couple weeks to work it out with HR and get senior management's approval," she told him. "Don't worry about anything. This *will* work out. Lauren and Beth will make a strong case for you."

"I sure hope so," said Bob.

"Look, I know we have some problems right now," said Stacy. "But I am totally confident that Lauren and Beth have our backs. It's hard for them, too. But this whole situation will improve."

Bob took a deep breath and pushed his glasses up on his nose. "I like this place," he said. "But it's just not the same as it used to be."

"We're going to turn things around," Stacy promised. "I don't know how, but I know we can do it."

"Don't get me wrong. I'm not threatening to quit," said Bob. "And I sure hope I don't get fired either. It's just that, well, even though I am pretty slow on the e-mails, I do feel like I give 110 percent right now. But I don't know how much longer I can keep it up."

CHAPTER 4

Enabling High Levels of Performance from Engaged Employees

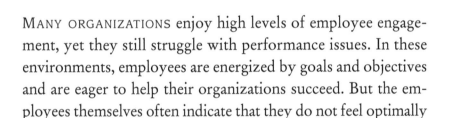

MANY ORGANIZATIONS enjoy high levels of employee engagement, yet they still struggle with performance issues. In these environments, employees are energized by goals and objectives and are eager to help their organizations succeed. But the employees themselves often indicate that they do not feel optimally productive.

Engaging employees, while clearly important, is not sufficient to sustain maximum levels of individual and team effectiveness over time.

What's the missing piece? To use a phrase made popular by the movie *Jerry Maguire*, engaged employees seem often to be saying to organizational leaders: "Help me help you." In other words: "Put us in roles that leverage our skills and abilities and allow us to do what we do best. Give us the tools, technology, information, support, and other resources we need to be effective. And, finally, get out of our way! Don't introduce procedural barriers that will interfere with our ability to get things done. And don't dilute our focus and consume our energy with tasks that don't add value."

Engagement Is Essential

Researchers have long recognized that organizations couldn't function through purely contractual relationships with employees. In the early twentieth century, for example, Chester Barnard, Elton Mayo, and others emphasized that organizations require *cooperation* from employees, not just compliance. Simple adherence to minimal role requirements is likely to have dysfunctional consequences in most settings. For example, unionized employees who "work to the rule" during contract disputes can quickly bring organizations to their knees.

In our view, "engagement" has captured the attention of managers insofar as it raises the notion of cooperation to a higher level. While cooperation is required and, to some extent, expected of all employees, engagement involves performing above and beyond what's expected. In that sense, engagement holds out to organizational leaders the prospect of increasing productivity (i.e., getting more output from a finite set of human capital resources).

In an environment of increasing competition and a challenging global economy, where organizations are running "leaner" and forced to do more with less, tapping into the discretionary effort offered by engaged employees becomes all the more imperative for success in the marketplace.

The ever-increasing pace of change in modern organizations also fosters interest in engagement. In fast-changing environments, it becomes all the more difficult to precisely specify roles and responsibilities across a diverse set of jobs. To the extent that employees at all levels are likely to be faced more frequently with unanticipated and ambiguous problem-solving and decision-making situations, employers must count on them to act on their own in ways that are consistent with company objectives based on their understanding of, and alignment with, organizational standards, cultures, and values.

A final push for today's emphasis on employee engagement comes from employees themselves. The redefinition of the social contract surrounding the employment relationship across all industries makes engagement a more pressing concern for many individuals. As the old loyalty-for-security bargain has eroded, the connections between individuals and organizations have grown more tenuous. Whereas a career was once defined as the steady movement over a period of time through a hierarchy of jobs in a single organization, individuals today are increasingly building careers from a series of patchwork moves across organizational boundaries. In charge of their own work paths, and with their own definitions of career success, more and more employees are looking for work environments where they can be engaged and feel that they are contributing in a positive way to something larger than themselves.

Though frameworks for understanding engagement vary, the concept is commonly understood to capture levels of commitment and discretionary effort exhibited by employees. Engaged employees can be expected to display high levels of attachment to an organization and a strong desire to remain a part of it. Consequently, engaged employees are more likely to be willing to go above and beyond the formal requirements of the job, contribute organizational citizenship behaviors, pour extra effort into their work, and deliver superior performance.

But Engagement Alone Is Not Enough

Hay Group research suggests that engaging employees, while important, is not sufficient to sustain maximum levels of performance over time. To get the most from employees, leaders must also ensure that organizational systems and work environments support personal and organizational effectiveness. They need not only to motivate their employees, but also to *enable* them to channel their extra efforts productively. As illustrated in the Bernette example, engaged employees need to have confidence that the organization is doing all it can to promote their success, rather than introducing barriers to getting their jobs done.

Employee enablement refers to the ability of individuals and teams that are already engaged to make maximum contributions. Enablement has two key components:

1. *Optimized roles* means that employees are effectively aligned with their positions, such that their skills and abilities are effectively put to good use. In deploying talent, leaders need to consider not only the requirements of the job and an employee's ability to meet them, but also the extent to which the job will draw upon and fully leverage the employee's distinctive competencies and aptitudes.

2. *A supportive environment* involves structuring work arrangements such that they facilitate, rather than hinder, individual productivity. In a supportive environment, employees have the essential resources (e.g., information, technology, tools and equipment, and financial support) required to get the job done. And they are able to focus on their most important

accountabilities without having to work around obstacles in the form of nonessential tasks or procedural red tape.

Figure 4.1 depicts a model of employee effectiveness that incorporates employee engagement as well as organizational supports for employees to be successful.

"Where there is a will, there is a way," goes the old saying. But our research confirms that employee engagement and employee enablement do not always go hand in hand. As we have seen, in many of today's organizations employees are highly committed to goals and objectives and are sincere in their desire to do the best job possible. Yet they are confronted with significant barriers to executing their job responsibilities efficiently and with high quality.

To the extent that their employees are presented with this frustration, organizations fail to harness the potential energy represented by employees who are engaged in their work.

Figure 4.1. Employee effectiveness framework.

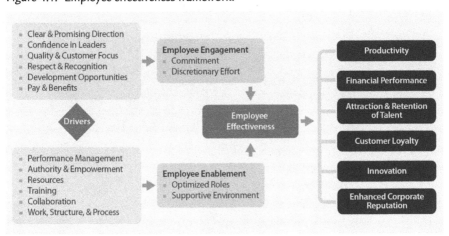

In most organizations, we can identify a group of employees who are both highly engaged and well enabled for success (the cell labeled "Effective" in Figure 4.2). In these happy instances, where motivation to contribute is matched with the ability to be successful, employees are likely to be high performers. Unfortunately, however, we also regularly find a set of employees lacking on both dimensions. Where both engagement and enablement are missing, employees are understandably likely to struggle in their job roles (the cell labeled "Ineffective").

Equally interesting, however, are the remaining cells. In most organizations we find a sizeable percentage of the population that falls into the "Detached" group. These employees are in roles that suit them reasonably well, and they find themselves in work environments that are generally supportive. But for various reasons, their levels of engagement with organizational objectives and task requirements are insufficient to make them optimally effective.

Figure 4.2. Workforce segmentation.

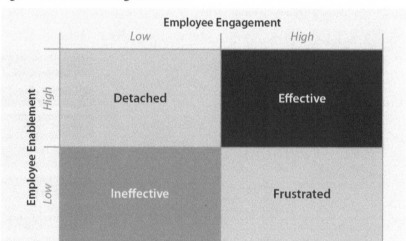

The real power of our framework comes in calling attention to the "Frustrated" employees in the bottom right corner of Figure 4.2. Based on our research, we believe that many organizations employ a significant number of people who are aligned with the direction of the organization and enthusiastic about making a difference, but are nonetheless held back by roles that do not suit them or work environments that get in their way. These employees represent a lost opportunity for organizations. From a motivational perspective, organizational leaders have these employees where they want them. But when it comes to getting the most from them in terms of productivity, employers have yet to leverage their full potential.

In fact, a lack of enablement for the employee who is engaged may be a bigger problem than the lack of engagement for the enabled employee. Again, think about Beth and Lauren at Bernette. They are frustrated because they care about the bank's success, its customers' satisfaction, and its reputation in the industry. If they weren't committed and engaged, they likely would not be so concerned about their inability to perform their jobs as effectively as they know to be possible.

Professor Thomas Britt of Clemson University and his colleagues have explored, in the context of military roles, the negative consequences of high levels of engagement when individuals face significant challenges to getting their jobs done effectively. In a survey of 1,200 U.S. Army rangers, Britt and his colleagues found, not surprisingly, that obstacles to high performance such as work overload resulted in lower levels of morale and job satisfaction. Notably, however, these effects were greatest for the most highly engaged soldiers. Indeed, "the most committed and personally invested rangers, the ones who ranked work-relevant values as the most important, ranked morale and job satisfaction lower in the face of insurmountable impediments. Simply put, the rangers who cared most about their work were the most demoralized when they were thwarted from doing their best." Along with the negative consequences of a lack of employee enablement for the motivation of highly engaged individuals, Britt also points to the likelihood of increased turnover. "For these high performers," he argues, "factors they can't control—role ambiguity, inadequate resources, and overwork itself—can hinder their best work and drive them to seek jobs elsewhere. The ones who stay behind may well be the ones who just don't care."[1]

The Role of Managers vs. Leaders

By focusing exclusively on employee engagement and ignoring employee enablement, organizations are likely to neglect key factors that impact the effectiveness of individuals and teams. As a result, engagement surveys may fail to identify the most critical improvement opportunities. What's most likely to be overlooked? While the predictors of engagement tend to reflect issues traditionally associated with leadership, the drivers of enablement relate directly to the quality of management in the organization.

Harvard professor John Kotter, in his 1990 *Harvard Business Review* article "What Leaders Really Do," suggested that key functions of a leader include:

- ▶ *Setting a direction* for the organization by creating a vision of the future

---

1. Thomas W. Britt, "Black Hawk Down at Work," *Harvard Business Review*, January 2003.

> ► *Ensuring alignment* at all levels by communicating the direction and fostering buy-in from managers and employees
>
> ► *Motivating and inspiring* by ensuring that managers and employees have faith in organizational objectives and confidence in the organization's ability to achieve them[2]

These functions align closely with the drivers of engagement identified in our research, particularly establishing a clear and promising direction and instilling confidence in the senior team.

In contrast, the drivers of employee enablement relate more directly to behaviors that have traditionally been associated with management rather than leadership. According to Kotter, these include:

> ► *Planning* (setting targets, formulating detailed plans, and allocating resources), relating in the context of our framework to performance management and the availability of resources to get the job done
>
> ► *Organizing and staffing* (creating appropriate authority structures, selecting and training people, and delegating responsibility), relating to authority and empowerment and training
>
> ► *Controlling and problem solving* (identifying and correcting deviations from plans), relating again to performance management

---

2. John P. Kotter, "What Leaders Really Do," *Harvard Business Review*, December 2001 (reprinted from the 1990 article).

Our employee effectiveness approach highlights the distinction between leadership and management and, most important, demonstrates the urgency of both for individual and team performance.

Interestingly, when Kotter and other theorists were writing in the late 1980s and early 1990s, they argued for an increased focus on leadership to counterbalance the heavy emphasis at the time on managerial behaviors. Notably, however, Kotter and others stressed that both were necessary for optimal organizational performance. As Kotter wrote, "While improving their ability to lead, companies should remember that strong leadership with weak management is no better, and is sometimes actually worse, than the reverse. The real challenge is to combine strong leadership and strong management and use each to balance the other."[3]

Unfortunately, the pendulum has swung in more recent years to an equally excessive focus on leadership in executive assessment and development programs. Many have overlooked the importance of solid management, as a complement to effective leadership, for the success of an organization.

We would argue that a better balance between management and leadership (i.e., between the strategic and operational aspects of the organization) must be achieved. Modern organizations need to celebrate both strong leadership *and* strong management, because both drive organizational performance over time. Our employee effectiveness framework, by focusing not only on employee engagement but also employee enablement, gives equal emphasis to both competencies and offers the

---

3. Ibid.

prospect of a more complete and more balanced perspective on important dynamics in the work environment.

The Right Balance

Our research with hundreds of companies shows just how critical employee engagement can be to an organization's success when combined with appropriate levels of employee enablement:

► Companies in the top quartile on engagement demonstrate revenue growth two and a half times that of organizations in the bottom quartile. But companies in the top quartile on both engagement and enablement achieve revenue growth four and a half times greater. To quantify the impact, consider an industry with average revenue growth of 8 percent. A typical company with $5 billion in revenues would see revenues increase by $400 million. A company with top quartile levels of employee engagement could expect an increase of $1 billion. And a company in the top quartile on both engagement and enablement could anticipate an increase of a full $1.8 billion!

► Companies in the top quartile on both engagement and enablement also exceed, by 40 percent to 60 percent, industry averages on five-year return on assets, return on investment, and return on equity.

► Companies with high levels of engagement show turnover rates 40 percent lower than companies with low levels of engagement. But companies that both engage and enable employees demonstrate a total reduction in voluntary turnover of 54 percent. Hay Group studies estimate the cost of replacing employees to be between 50 percent and 150 percent of salary. For an organization with twenty thousand employees and an annual voluntary turnover rate of 8 percent, the cost of turnover is approximately $56 million (assuming an average salary of $35,000 and an average replacement cost of 100 percent of salary). Reducing the voluntary turnover rate by 40 percent would yield annual savings of $22.4 million. But reductions in turnover through higher levels of engagement and enablement would yield savings of more than $30 million annually—a difference of more than $7.5 million.

▶ Our research linking employee survey data to performance ratings shows that highly engaged employees are 10 percent more likely to exceed performance expectations. But highly engaged *and* enabled employees are 50 percent more likely to outperform expectations. Past studies have shown that the difference in productivity between superior and typical performers is 35 percent on average, depending on job complexity.[4] For an organization producing $10 billion of product with 20 percent of employees exceeding performance expectations, increasing the percentage of high performers by one and a half times (by transforming average performers into superior ones) would increase output by $350 million.

The bottom line: Highly engaged and enabled workers create dramatically better business outputs, more loyal customers, and better financial performance during good times and bad. And organizations are likely to retain these employees and sustain these results.

---

4. J. E. Hunter, F. L. Schmidt, and M. K. Judiesch (1990), "Individual Differences in Output Variability as a Function of Job Complexity," *Journal of Applied Psychology* 75: 28–42.

⯈ Deeper Dive: How Most Admired Companies Use Enablement in Strategy Execution

Hay Group has partnered with *Fortune* magazine annually since 1997 to identify the World's Most Admired Companies and uncover the business practices that make these companies both highly regarded and highly successful. Our studies have focused on a wide range of topics, including attraction and retention of talent, leadership development, performance management, corporate culture, innovation, and effectiveness in conducting business globally.

Over the course of our research, we have found again and again that Most Admired Companies are better able to carry out strategies, deliver on goals and plans, and generally get things done. Notably, knowledge of best practices is not what determines competitive success for companies but rather the ability to successfully implement and sustain these practices. Most executives, consultants, and academics can readily point to the right things to do. What separates great companies from others is the ability to make the ideal real. A. G. Lafley, former CEO of Procter & Gamble, observed, "It's not a secret what needs to be done. The challenge is to put the strategy, systems, and capabilities in place and then drive deployment and execution." Our findings confirm that enablement factors are key to the success of Most Admired Companies in executing their strategies where many others fail, particularly managing performance and managing interdependencies.

Managing Performance

As Larry Bossidy and Ram Charan noted in their bestselling book *Execution*, "Clear, simple goals don't mean much if nobody takes them seriously. The failure to follow through is widespread in business, and a major cause of poor execution."[5] Leaders in Most

---

5. L. Bossidy and R. Charan, *Execution: The Discipline of Getting Things Done* (New York: Crown Business, 2002).

Admired Companies, more so than in peer companies, reinforce the accountabilities of managers and employees by managing performance and following through consistently to ensure that people are able to do the things they commit to doing. In Most Admired Companies, managers are more likely to be held accountable for their roles in implementing strategies, and where they fall short, action to help them turn around their performance is more likely to be taken.

Most Admired Companies encourage managers to focus on the accountabilities most critical for business success by tying performance measures directly to business strategies and linking compensation to the achievement of performance objectives. Managers in Most Admired Companies view their performance measures as more challenging than managers in peer companies. But, perhaps attesting to their confidence in their ability to execute, leaders in Most Admired Companies also tend to see their performance measures as clearer and more realistic.

While managers in all companies report that performance measures encourage a focus on the numbers (e.g., growth, profitability), the performance management systems of Most Admired Companies are distinctive in emphasizing to a much greater degree the importance of building customer loyalty and building human capital. As such, performance goals in Most Admired Companies tend to be more forward looking. As is often said, if you want to know where a company is now, look at the financials. But if you want to know where a company will be in five to ten years, look at the quality of its customer relationships and the quality of its talent. Similarly, managers in Most Admired Companies are much more likely than their peers to report that their performance goals encourage them to balance long-term objectives with quarter-to-quarter demands.

Designing effective performance management systems can be particularly challenging in global companies, given the diverse and at times competing goals of managers across business units and subsidiaries. Most global companies don't operate simply as a portfolio of businesses, but rather look to exploit the interdependencies and synergies across businesses. Because the success of one business unit is often dependent on the success of others, it can be hard to provide accurate assessments of how well managers in particular business units or subsidiaries are doing. Similarly, the objectives of local units may not always be aligned with those of the broader enterprise. Managing a global organization has been likened to a game of global chess, with senior leaders aiming to move pieces to position the overall organization optimally. But just as pawns may have to be sacrificed in chess to move the game forward, it may sometimes be in the interest to the broader enterprise for a local business unit or subsidiary to depress its performance for a period of time. A global company might, for instance, have a strategic interest in putting cost pressures on one of its competitors in the competitor's home market. That may hurt the local subsidiary in the short term but benefit the broader enterprise in the long run.

Most Admired Companies report greater success with both of these aspects of performance management. They are more confident that performance management systems facilitate the success of local managers in achieving their objectives. And the performance management systems of Most Admired Companies are also reported to be more effective in focusing managers on enterprise-wide objectives and encouraging managers in business units or subsidiaries to sacrifice local priorities where necessary to benefit the global enterprise.

Clarity and consistency are key components of the performance management and compensation approaches of Most Admired Companies. These companies are more likely than their peers to indicate that they have clearly defined global approaches to performance management and compensation that are centralized (emphasizing internal consistency) rather than decentralized (emphasizing flexibility in local labor markets). "Caterpillar evaluates and measures performance the same way around the world," observed group president Stuart Levenick. "This is true for succession planning as well. Using the same performance measures, we are able to assess our talent and place individuals in positions around the world that work for the company and the individuals' career growth."

Managing Interdependencies

Through flatter structures, broader roles, and the use of teams, many organizations have created significant "white space" between business units and functions. As organizations have become more complex, decision making has become more complex and often more problematic. Whereas once people were likely to have had either sole ownership for a decision or responsibility for contributing to it, in today's organizations there are more situations where both decisions and accountabilities are shared. In these cases, the role an individual or a function plays in the decision-making process needs to be explicit, or else the lack of clarity may result in conflict, gridlock, or lost opportunities.

Most Admired Companies indicate that decision-making accountabilities and processes are better defined than those of their peers, making it clearer who should have input into decisions and who is primarily accountable for making them. And they are also more positive than their peers regarding the extent to which decision-making processes and reporting relationships promote timely decision making.

Managing interdependencies in an organization also requires performance management systems that provide incentives to cooperate. Notably, managers in Most Admired Companies are much more likely than managers in other organizations to indicate that performance measures encourage collaboration. In one particularly strong example, there was an interesting twist built into the executive team incentive program. The system was structured such that leaders could not meet their personal targets on their own. Not only did the organization need to meet its numbers and individuals need to accomplish their goals, but a full payout required that each and every individual on the leadership team made his or her numbers. The message: "We're all in this together. Even if the company succeeds and you succeed personally, you are tied to your colleagues' success as well."

Firms operating internationally confront special challenges in coordinating operations across a far-flung set of business units and subsidiaries. Procedural systems are essential (e.g., accounting and auditing systems, policies and procedures). But global organizations are unlikely to be able to rely on them exclusively, given the complexity associated with diverse markets. Accordingly, "normative" control systems, emphasizing consensus on a broader set of corporate objectives, are a critical complement to formal approaches. The importance of alignment in coordinating operations is clearly acknowledged by Novartis. "We recognize the challenges of operating globally," notes Novartis chairman Dr. Daniel Vasella. "We have units which are geographic, units which are functional, and project organizations. So the question is 'what does everybody have in common?' And how can we strengthen this and communicate this? What we have in common is primarily the purpose of the company."

Most Admired Companies are more likely to report that they have succeeded in aligning their various business units and subsidiaries around a common strategic vision and around a common corporate culture. Most Admired Companies are also more effective in communicating changes in strategic direction and corporate policies and procedures to business unit and subsidiary managers.

Most Admired Companies have in place the right goals—goals that focus on the measures that lead to success. They also have in place the right processes that enable leaders, managers, and employees to reach those goals.

Nonfinancial Impacts of Engagement and Enablement

In Chapter 3 we met Stacy Robbins, a longtime Bernette employee. Stacy is a call center shift supervisor whose frustration is mounting. Among Stacy's concerns (which are shared by her boss, Lauren, and others in the organization) is the need to work longer and longer hours to accomplish the same tasks that she used to be able to do in less time. U.S. Bureau of Labor Statistics data indicate that by 1999 nearly 30 percent of all managers and professionals were working forty-nine or more hours per week, with the number rising to roughly 40 percent among male managers and professionals.[6] Couple that trend with the prevalence of two-career families and you have a recipe for work-life balance concerns. Estimates also suggest that the pool of U.S. workers between the ages of 35 and 44 will shrink by 7 percent between 2002 and 2012.[7]

Complicating matters further, employees' work schedules are becoming increasingly erratic. According to the Current Population Survey (a collaborative effort between the Bureau of Labor Statistics and the Census Bureau), by 2004 about 20 percent of employed Americans were working evenings, overnight, or on rotating shifts.[8] And even for those working more traditional hours, operating in a global economy and high-technology society often means extending the workday

---

6. "Are Managers and Professionals Really Working More?" *Issues in Labor Statistics*, U.S. Department of Labor Bureau of Labor Statistics, May 2000.

7. *Occupational Outlook Quarterly* 47, no. 4 (Winter 2003–2004). With millions of baby boomers poised to retire, many organizations will face an acute talent crunch that can be expected to place increased demands on existing staff.

8. T. McMenamin, "A Time to Work: Recent Trends in Shift Work and Flexible Schedules," *Monthly Labor Review*, December 2007.

to accommodate clients and colleagues several time zones apart.

How are organizations responding to increased work-life balance concerns? Typical approaches have been tactical, seeking to provide employees with more flexibility in where and when they work. Organizations have emphasized telecommuting options, flexible work schedules, compressed workweeks, on-site daycare, and other similar benefits. While these are certainly helpful, we believe that they fail to address the fundamental problem: Professional and personal demands simply leave today's maxed-out workers with too much to do and too little time to do it.

Given that time available for work is finite and work demands are unlikely to decrease anytime soon, long-term solutions to work-life balance issues also need to focus on helping employees work more productively. By providing strong employee enablement in the work environment, organizations can help employees accomplish work tasks as efficiently as possible, leaving more time to attend to personal responsibilities.

To explore the relationships between employee enablement and work-life balance, we examined Hay Group employee opinion data to isolate a best-practice group of organizations that scored in the top quartile on employees' ratings of their sensitivity to work-life balance concerns. We compared these with organizations scoring in the bottom quartile on this issue, examining a wide range of workplace practices.

The results suggest that organizations need to focus on more than just flexible work schedules and telecommuting programs to help employees manage work and personal responsibilities. The organizations that are judged by employees to be most sensitive to their personal lives effectively manage a broader set of workplace dynamics. Specifically, these "work-life balance leaders":

- ► Provide clear direction regarding organizational priorities to help employees focus on the highest-value tasks
- ► Implement policies and practices consistently to ensure that workloads are fairly and equitably distributed
- ► Emphasize high levels of teamwork within and across organizational units to provide employees with access to support from coworkers in coping with work demands
- ► Support training, development, and empowerment opportunities to ensure that employees at all levels have the skills and decision-making authority to get the job done
- ► Provide adequate resources (e.g., tools, equipment, supplies) to enable employees to execute work tasks efficiently and with high quality

These results suggest that many of the factors that are associated with a more effective and enabled workforce also lead to work environments where employees are more positive about stress and work-life balance issues. By permitting employees to complete the most vital tasks as efficiently as possible, organizations with supportive environments limit the extent to which work tasks "crowd out" personal time. At the same time, even when workloads are heavy, employees are likely to feel far better about staying late or coming in early if they are working on tasks with a clear and compelling purpose, provided with adequate resources and support from colleagues, and given the authority necessary to make decisions about how best to accomplish their objectives.

One U.S.-based financial services and insurance firm we worked with recently used a comprehensive employee opinion survey to better understand the drivers of work-life balance. To explore these issues, employees were segmented based on their reported levels of engagement and enablement. Employees were classified as *effective* (high levels of both engagement and enablement), *detached* (low levels of engagement, high levels of enablement), *frustrated* (high levels of engagement, low levels of enablement), or *ineffective* (low levels of both engagement and enablement). The relationships between engagement, enablement, and work-life balance issues related to stress on the job were readily evident:

- ► *Effective* employees were 82 percent favorable regarding the amount of stress they experience at work.
- ► *Detached* employees were 73 percent favorable.
- ► *Frustrated* employees were 62 percent favorable.
- ► *Ineffective* employees were 44 percent favorable.

The organization felt it was in its best interest to take action on departments with large numbers of *frustrated* employees and understand the barriers they faced in their work. Employees in these departments reported lack of training for specific responsibilities, inefficient workflow, poor communication within and between departments, and inadequate performance feedback from supervisors. Taking steps to address concerns in these areas not only helped mitigate the stress and work-life balance issues faced by these employees, but also helped them feel better supported to be successful in their work and, therefore, more productive.

When Enablement Trumps Engagement

There is no job or work environment where higher levels of engagement will not create higher chances of superior performance. Thus, managers, with the present focus on employee engagement, are led to view higher levels of engagement as the recipe for improved performance in roles of all types. As the old saying goes, when you have a hammer everything looks like a nail. But it is important to recognize that there are particular types of jobs in organizations where enablement can be far more important than engagement. While employee engagement is clearly beneficial in most contexts, it may be less important than organizational support, depending on the role.

In highly routinized jobs, such as assembly line work, enablement factors—such as the quality of employee training, the efficiency with which work is structured, and the adequacy of tools and technology—may be expected to have a bigger effect on employee output than motivation levels. From an organizational perspective, support may also be particularly critical in roles where high levels of turnover are expected—hourly staff in retail and hospitality industries, for instance, or at the Bernette call center, where turnover, while historically low compared to that of the rest of the industry, is still relatively high compared to that of organizations outside the financial services sector. After all, when employees leave they take their engagement out the door with them, but a supportive work environment remains as an organizational asset.

Enablement may emerge as a stronger differentiator of performance in some industries than others as well. There are certain companies where high levels of employee engagement can be expected due to a strong brand. The challenge, then, is not to create engagement, but to channel it. The issue is particularly important for companies in the communications, media, and technology (CMT) sector. These companies, with their "hot" (or "cool") images and sexy products, typically find it easier to engage their people. In effect, we could call these people "auto-engaged."

The CMT industry is full of compelling brands that give people pride and passion about working for their employers. Who would not want to work for a trendy magazine, a funky telecom supplier, or an innovative and design-led technology business? If you are feeling disengaged, just go to the newsstand and read one of your own articles (that fifty thousand other people are reading), go to one of your retail outlets and drool over the cool stuff you make, or listen to the buzz generated by your latest product launch. Many CMT employees simply enjoy their work and solving the technical challenges that come with the job.

Given the auto-engagement phenomenon, the role of managers in the CMT industry is subtly different from that in other industries. CMT organizations are luckier than many: they already have lots of people wanting to go the extra mile. These organizations need their managers to make employees more productive by enabling them to direct all their extra effort productively.

Managers in these settings who focus exclusively on engagement are arguably not doing their jobs properly. Instead of trying to enhance morale and motivation levels, they should help their teams to be productive by creating the conditions for success, by removing organizational barriers, by getting support from other parts of the business, and by making sure that their teams are aligned with organizational goals.

Enablement: Essential for Sustaining Performance Over Time

Enablement is key not only to generating high levels of organizational performance, but also to sustaining it. An organization may be able to succeed by the force of will of motivated employees in the short term, but over the long haul adequate support is necessary to avoid burnout. Consider a case-study example: For a major UK retailer, we linked employee engagement and employee enablement across approximately five hundred stores with store-level measures of customer satisfaction and fiscal year revenue against target, collected at two different points in time. Employee engagement and employee enablement were both associated with more favorable customer and financial outcomes. But after a six-month lag, enablement was a much stronger driver.

Positioning employees to succeed is also critical to retaining them over the long term. For a leading financial services firm, we related employee engagement and employee enablement levels to actual employee departures in the twelve months following an employee opinion survey. Notably, while engagement and enablement were both strong predictors of turnover in the first two quarters, enablement was a much more important determinant of attrition in the third and fourth quarters.

Call it "enablement," call it "support for success," or call it "doing the job of a manager properly." The key is helping teams to channel their energy into organizational goals, so that it doesn't fade away. Bernette employees are beginning to feel that they can't carry on much longer without increased support. Few frustrated employees do.

CHAPTER 5

Doing More with Less

"Smile!"

The half-dozen newly minted Bernette call center reps crowded themselves into the frame. A second later, Stacy Robbins, their shift supervisor, snapped their picture. It was a typical ending to a typical two-week training and orientation. In fifteen minutes, the members of the smiling group would be taking their first calls. Their training complete, Beth came around to meet each one and extend a warm welcome.

Stacy had already told Beth and Lauren that this was a particularly bright, interesting group of trainees. When Beth told them, "Welcome to Bernette, we are so happy you are here!" she meant it.

Stacy led the group from the break room where they were congregated into the call center, where their workstations awaited them. "I didn't think we'd be rolling this fast!" exclaimed one of the group, a college student named Dan who'd been hired on a part-time basis. "At my last job, we had to sit around for two days after training while they got our company IDs and workstations ready for us." Stacy noted an excitement in Dan's voice. He was eager to start. The orientation—with its Bernette-branded emphasis on the bank's mission and the opportunities it offered to employees—had obviously had an effect. The entire group, Stacy noted, was enthusiastic. This was not unusual. Bernette's orientation program always did a great job of selling the organization to new employees.

As Stacy was leading the group into the call center, she turned and saw Beth watching them. She couldn't help but notice a faint look of resignation on Beth's face, a tiny, nearly imperceptible expression of regret. When Beth saw that Stacy was watching her, she turned the look into a warm smile. But when her eyes met Stacy's, each knew what the other was thinking: *Sure, everyone's excited on day one. But how long will it last?*

After the new reps got their start, Stacy returned to her desk to post the group pictures to the bank's internal website. Looking over the photos of Bernette employees—on the job, at company picnics, volunteering at homeless shelters—she was stung by something she saw: a photo of a smiling Ray Pough. When Stacy was hired, Ray had been her manager, but within a couple of years he was promoted to the executive team. The photo was taken more than a year ago at the bank's annual meeting. Only a few weeks after the meeting, Bernie had announced the upcoming merger with Green Tree. Stacy studied Ray's face. She guessed he knew about the merger at the time. And she knew that at his level, it could take a year to find a new position in the industry. So, she surmised, when this photograph was taken, Ray might have already decided that he was going to resign. Nothing in his face betrayed it. He was surrounded by his staff, their arms wrapped around one another for the shot.

Stacy studied the photos. A year from now, would a fast-rising rep (perhaps from the group she'd oriented that day) be sitting at this same desk, posting pictures of new employees and wondering why Stacy had left the bank?

She pushed the thought out of her head and posted the new photos.

Stacy Robbins began working at Bernette Financial before the bank even had a call center. She started out as a part-time teller during her senior year of high school. After a few months, she decided she liked working at Bernette. Most of her friends had jobs at fast-food restaurants. They came home smelling like grease and complaining about their managers. But Stacy thrived in a professional environment. The work was detail-oriented and demanding, but she was good at it.

Today, sitting at her desk, she thought again about her own interview fifteen years earlier. On that day, when she was in the lobby of the bank's fourth-floor office, waiting for the HR person to bring her in, Stacy was keenly aware of the positive feeling in the air. Whatever it was, Bernette was a special place. It made an impression on her. The tellers seemed so happy to serve their customers, as though they were on a mission, she thought.

During the interview, Stacy made sure to mention that not only had she done babysitting as a teenager, but she had organized a network of sitters—all of whom agreed to take Red Cross CPR training—to better serve parents in her suburban Denver neighborhood. "So, even though this will be my first actual job," she explained, "I do have management experience and an entrepreneurial personality."

Stacy was hired after HR checked her references. She worked on Friday nights, Saturdays, and Wednesdays after school, about fifteen hours a week. HR, Ray Pough, and eventually the founder and CEO himself could not help but notice Stacy's tremendous poise, her professionalism, and her friendly nature. Plus she was a quick study who took it upon herself to keep abreast of new products and services so she could be proactive in helping customers choose among the bank's many offerings.

Stacy was a natural-born optimist, always seeing the bright side and rarely taking things personally. She was always helpful to customers, even when they were unpleasant or demanding.

One day as he was making his rounds, Bernie Ellsworth observed Stacy doing a great job handling a customer dispute. The customer didn't have proper identification, and Stacy didn't recognize her. The customer was livid. She wanted her money! Stacy offered solution after solution until the customer agreed to call her daughter and ask her to bring the necessary identification to the bank.

Afterward, Bernie called Ray Pough aside and asked, "What is that young lady's customer service secret? I want to bottle it! She's unflappable."

Ray smiled and confessed he had asked her the same question only a week earlier, after she'd resolved a similar dispute with a particularly unpleasant customer. "I asked her how she managed to remain so calm under fire, and you know what she said? She told me that she always tried to feel sorry for customers who were verbally abusive. She said she feels for them because they're unhappy, and that keeps her from getting angry at them." Bernie shook his head in disbelief. "She's wise for her age," he said.

⌐

Ten months after Stacy started at Bernette, she graduated from Cherry Creek West High School. Six weeks before graduation, the bank made Stacy a formal offer: full-time work as head teller beginning three weeks after graduation. She accepted the offer and enrolled part-time at the University of Denver. With three girlfriends, Stacy enjoyed a two-week road trip in a 1968 Pontiac Firebird convertible. They drove west across the Rocky Mountains, spent a few days visiting the Grand Canyon, then continued west and drove up the coast highway from Los Angeles to San Francisco. They stopped at Big Sur to walk along the coast, talk about their futures, and watch the mighty Pacific Ocean. It was on that trip that she began to think she wanted a career doing work that meant something, that helped people, and that could afford her vacations like that.

Early that July, Stacy began her career full-time with Bernette Financial. Two years later, when the online division was started up, Ray was promoted to the senior team and Stacy made the move to the call center with the understanding that after gaining experience as a call center representative, she would be promoted to supervisor—the youngest manager in the bank's history—in charge of daily operations.

Stacy was the pride and joy of the call center, fresh and charming, calm and professional, highly knowledgeable about the bank's products, and loyal to an organization that took a chance on a girl with "advanced babysitting experience," as she liked to joke.

Stacy became the go-to person when someone from marketing or IT needed to shepherd a project through the call center. She knew the systems; she knew the bank's products; she knew its customers; and, most important, she cared. Stacy poured her heart into her work. And it showed. Her contributions were noted. And her reward? A rapid ascent, a bright future, and the confidence of her employer. Now that she had her college degree, not to mention that she was taking classes toward her MBA, there was no stopping Stacy. She'd work her way to the top. She didn't mind putting in long hours, especially since her children were now in school and her husband worked at home as a systems analyst for a software developer. She'd get a seat at the table. She'd enjoy the privileges of senior management, maybe one day a corner office. She'd achieve all that!

But lately, for the first time in fifteen years, Stacy had begun to think that she might end up achieving all of that at another bank.

In her heart, Stacy felt like Bernette was still a great place to work. The people were terrific and the mission hadn't changed since she first arrived. But these days it was a lot harder to get things done.

Stacy was realistic; with growth comes change. She was prepared for that. But, perhaps because she'd been there so long, she had begun to notice a few changes that concerned her, not the least of which was her old boss's sudden and unexplained departure.

Another change Stacy didn't like was feeling like she was walking on eggshells around Lauren and Beth. The other day, Stacy mentioned to Lauren that she had never been busier now that she was managing reps on two different CRMs. "I don't know how I can keep up the service levels when more and more work keeps being added but we're not being given tools to do the job right." Lauren just looked annoyed. Stacy began to apologize. "I didn't mean to complain, Lauren, it's just that—"

Lauren cut her off. "I know. You're being forced to do more with less. That's the new mantra around here. Didn't you get the memo?" Lauren tried to couch her remark as a joke, but the frustration in her voice was unmistakable. "Sorry," she said. "I didn't mean to snap at you, but we're going to have to rise to the occasion."

Lauren wasn't the only manager who seemed discouraged lately. Beth too was spending more time in her office, less time walking the floor, and less time smiling. Stacy had also noted that April Fool's Day came and went with no one getting a phony phone call from Bernie, no company-wide announcements of fake activities like last year's "Everyone in the parking lot for a round of loaded suitcase catching. The suitcase droppers have taken their places on the roof of the building."

Two days later, Stacy poked her head into Lauren's office and tapped lightly on the door frame. "Just wanted to let you know that the new crew of reps is off to a great start," she said. "By the way, did Beth make any headway with HR about getting Bob his transfer?"

Lauren spun around on her office chair and gave Stacy a look that said everything. Stacy entered her boss's office, flopped herself into the spare chair, and pouted like a recalcitrant teenager. "Aw, Lauren . . . !" she began.

But Lauren shut her down with one index finger pointed in the younger woman's direction. "Don't whine," she said, pointing to the "No Whining Zone" plaque on her wall. The two shared a restrained smile.

"Bob is feeling really low," said Stacy. "I would never have told him about the plan to promote him if it hadn't seemed like a sure thing. I couldn't imagine it being held up, and especially for such a lame reason."

Lauren explained to Stacy exactly what Beth had told her:

"When the two banks merged, there was a lot of give-and-take, you know? The main goal was to shed as few jobs as possible. And we were pretty successful with that. The next goal is to integrate the banking systems, then the CRM systems. We're doing heavy lifting here, Stacy. And in a few months we'll be ready to take on the smaller aspects, like integrating the banks' policies and tossing out outdated ones that we don't need. And at that point, we can talk about dropping that old policy and getting Bob where he belongs."

"How long will it take?" Stacy asked. "Bob isn't going to sit around waiting for this transfer forever. Let's face it: He's on a performance improvement action plan because he's in the wrong job. And the beautiful thing is, we have the right job for him. Marketing needs him. In that role he is capable of delivering so much more!"

The Bob issue was one of several that were making it a challenge for Stacy to do her job effectively and efficiently. Another was the size of the teams. Stacy was responsible for coaching call center reps on her shift. But as the shift got bigger, it became increasingly harder to spend enough time with each rep during the shift. She felt as though she was shortchanging her reps. She didn't want to think about the bright, fresh new group she had just oriented getting burned out. She would have liked to spend more time coaching them, but there *was* no time.

"Lauren," said Stacy, feeling brave. "You're trained in engineering, right?"

"Close," said Lauren. "Industrial design."

Stacy nodded her head. "Good enough. Okay, so please talk me through doing more with less like it was a project or a design concept or something. Show me how it works."

Lauren smirked. "Very funny. You know that's impossible, and you know what I mean by doing more with less."

Stacy stood firm. "No, I don't. I'm serious," she said. "Imagine a ten-person crew building a house. They have a certain number of days to do it. Now two of the workers call in sick, and there are no replacements. They'll each miss two days of work. But the remaining workers are told that they'll still have to complete the job on time. They may grumble. But they can do it even if they're two men short. They can work an hour extra a day, or come in on a weekend. But . . . say two workers get sick and they take the tools home with them. No hammers. No nails, no ladders or saws. And there's no budget to go out and buy new tools. Now if the contractor tells the workers they still have to complete the task on time with no tools, they will think he's out of his mind. And if he insists, they can try, but they'll fail. Because without the tools, this crew can't get its job done. And that's how it's beginning to feel around here. We want to do our best, but we can't. And who wants to settle?"

Another one of Stacy's jobs was to analyze escalated calls so Bernette could understand how to handle these calls more effectively when they first come in. Bernette's first-call-resolved target was 75 percent, meaning that three-quarters of all first-time calls are resolved by the rep handling the call. Reducing the volume of escalated calls was of enormous importance. Escalations take time. If a handful of escalations per shift could be resolved by the initial rep—and avoid escalation—that would go a long way toward improving the call center's service levels.

The problem was that escalations had hit the roof over the past few months. Because of the CRM issues, all too often reps couldn't find the information they needed to resolve the call on their monitors, so they'd walk the floors in search of a rep with a CRM with the right information. For example, Green Tree used to sell and service two types of college tuition savings plans, one for students attending in-state colleges, and one for those attending out-of-state. The two plans had different rules for tax purposes. Bernette, on the other hand, offered only one plan. So whenever a Bernette call center rep took a call about one of Green Tree's tuition-saving products, he or she had to find a rep with a "Green Tree terminal" who wasn't on the phone to get the answer. And as everyone who has ever interacted with a call center knows, no customer calls because he wants to sit on hold. No one likes listening to canned music interrupted by a recorded voice announcing that "your call is important to us."

The CRM problem was driving down service levels, and it was frustrating Stacy and the people around her. "Like I said, Lauren, I don't want to make it sound like all I do is complain, and this isn't a complaint, it's a serious question. I mean, hypothetically, how would that construction crew do more with less? What would it look like?"

Lauren had no answer. She sat quietly, waiting for Stacy to make her point.

"And how do my reps resolve a pretty simple call in one minute when they have to walk for a minute and a half to find the information they need?"

Lauren took her time. She didn't want to upset Stacy any more than she already had. "Beth had a talk with Angela about this," she said. "She expressed these concerns to her, and Angela is aware of them."

"Let me guess," said Stacy. "I bet she was told it's 'crunch time.'"

A bit exasperated, Lauren nodded. She had to admit that "crunch time" was the exact phrase Beth had related to her.

Stacy continued. "Everyone is being asked to do more with less. I understand. But 'do more with less' shouldn't be just an empty phrase. In some contexts, sure, you can do more with less, like the construction crew that's two guys short. But it can't work in every situation, and it's not working here. We're doing less with less."

Another frustration: The bank's marketing group would at times change a feature of one of the bank's products and forget to notify Beth in the call center. It was Beth's job to bring the new data to Lauren, who would then work with IT to get the information into the CRMs so that the reps could access it. And it was up to Stacy to conduct product training with the reps. Sometimes an upgrade was easy to implement. Other times it required more time and knowledge. But Lauren was incapable of making these changes and alerting Stacy and the reps when no one told her about them.

Stacy was beginning to sound like a broken record. "We need tools and resources to do our jobs, Lauren."

Fifteen years ago Stacy was voted Most Perky in her high school class. These days, however, she felt more put upon than perky. It was overwhelming to have to react to last-minute training needs and changes in scheduling while supervising a shift, monitoring calls, and assisting Lauren with forecasts and scheduling.

When the call center first opened, Stacy worked with IT to create an onboarding plan, a system for bringing new people into the organization. "Not Your Mama's Orientation" was the nickname for the program. The goal was to get each and every new call center employee up and working as quickly as possible after training. At other banks, there was often a delay in getting a new workstation set up. But by coordinating with HR and IT, Stacy managed to get people seated and working soon after completing their training. She read some articles about onboarding. She made some calculations and discovered that if she could get every single new call center employee onboarded a half-day faster, Bernette would save nearly $100,000 a year. Besides, like the group Stacy had just brought in, new reps wanted to get on the phones as soon as they could and bring some of that vitality to the job.

Interestingly, this onboarding solution came to Stacy on her own time. But lately she wasn't much inclined to use her own time for work-related contemplation, planning, or problem solving. She just wasn't feeling much of a payoff for putting in that kind of effort. And even when she did try to solve a work-related problem during off hours, since the reorganization it often just involved how to play catch-up.

The lack of tools and resources slowed down everyone in the call center. Instead of thinking about innovations, she would think about workarounds. For example, when a rep who had no Green Tree data in her CRM got a call about a Green Tree product and had to walk down the hall to get the information from another rep, Stacy advised the rep to make a quick note on two or three other products that showed up on the colleague's monitor. That way, they could save a little time at the end of the day. But that wasn't a solution; it was a second-rate stopgap measure.

Stacy worried about the plunging service levels. First-time calls resolved had dropped from over 80 percent, an industry high, to around 65 percent, an unacceptable low. Customers

DOING MORE WITH LESS

hung up angry and dissatisfied. Some even withdrew their savings and went to another bank.

Stacy wondered to herself whether Ray Pough had resigned because he wanted to go out on top, when Bernette's numbers were good and the bank was still making news for being one of America's best places to work.

⌐⌐

Two weeks later, Stacy waited in a lobby for the interview she'd secured the week before. Though Stacy was in her early thirties, with a bachelor's degree and several credits toward her MBA, this was only her second job interview. The interviewer—Boulder Savings' HR director—seemed impressed by her accomplishments. He wanted to know why Stacy was thinking about leaving Bernette. "That place is famous for retention," he said. "Why are you looking elsewhere?"

Stacy respected the people at Bernette too much to criticize them, especially to a competitor. Plus, she didn't think it was appropriate to make negative comments about her current employer. She drew a deep breath and explained to her interviewer that she had been working for the same employer since high school. "As you can see, I'm working on my MBA, and I would really like to move up in this industry. I've spoken with a number of professionals, and most tell me it is a good idea to get a broad range of experience. I think having only one employer would limit me. I need to take in other perspectives and broaden my experience."

The interviewer seemed satisfied with Stacy's answer. After all, it made sense. But something nagged at Stacy. What she'd just said was reasonable; it wasn't untrue per se. But it wasn't really *her* answer. While it might have been a good idea to get more diverse experience elsewhere, she would have no desire to leave Bernette if things there were the way they used to be. She just couldn't do the quality of work that she knew she was capable of doing.

Stacy smiled and looked into the interviewer's eyes. "I feel so fortunate to have grown up at Bernette," she told him. "I've learned a lot from Bernie Ellsworth. He's a great role model."

When asked where she saw herself in ten years, Stacy had her answer prepared. "I see myself as a vice president," she said. "While I respect commercial lending, I see myself more on the individual consumer side, you know, helping families afford to send their kids to college or plan for retirement. I feel like bankers really get to help people in that role. My MBA will be in finance, and I feel that with my supervisory experience and my experience leading projects, I have something pretty special to offer."

The interviewer made a few notes on Stacy's résumé, and then he said, "I'm impressed. While I can't make any promises, I would like you to interview with our VP of operations. Are you free early next week?" Stacy scheduled her second interview and headed back to Bernette feeling ambivalent.

After pulling into the Bernette parking lot, back from her "doctor's appointment," Stacy sat in her car for a moment looking at the bank, its glass façade and its prominent "B.F." logo etched into the front window.

There was so much happening on the inside. Between the merger and the subsequent reorganization, it felt as though the call center was getting lost in the shuffle. The new reps she had trained a few weeks earlier were still enthusiastic. They'd met Bernie and Howard during one of their rare visits to the call center. As always, Bernie's joie de vivre was infectious. He loved life, he loved the banking business, and he loved the organization he had built. Howard made a great impression as well. Friendly, sincere, and obviously proud of his online vision, he inspired the new group of employees, each of whom was invited to step away from their terminals for the introductions. They shook hands with the current CEO and the future CEO as though they were meeting movie stars. After all, they'd read about Bernie and Howard in magazines. Even before they applied for their jobs, they'd heard about what a special place Bernette was. And just a few weeks into their tenure, their enthusiasm had yet to wane.

Stacy was torn. She still believed in Bernette, but she didn't know how much longer she could stick it out. With a sigh, she grabbed her pocketbook, got out of her car, and went into the bank. Once inside she went straight downstairs to the call center. In the elevator on the way down she took a couple deep breaths and reminded herself: *Perky, perky.*

CHAPTER 6

Engagement Walks in the Door and Trips over Enablement

As most of us know, and as illustrated by the "newbie" Bernette call center employees introduced in Chapter 5, there is a "tenure effect" at play in most organizations. Not surprisingly, surveys show that employee opinions about an organization are consistently most favorable among the newly hired.

Your relationship with an organization is like your relationship with a significant other. It begins with infatuation. Think about Stacy Robbins, fresh out of high school, hired by a bank that was famous for its goodwill and its family ownership—a bank with a great reputation as one of America's best places to work, where her parents had saved their money. Stacy wasn't just optimistic about her prospects at Bernette; she was practically in love with the place!

New employees are typically hopeful about (and open to) all the possibilities and potential represented by their new roles and the organization. But, as with romantic relationships, the initial glow cannot be sustained. If it's not replaced with a deeper, more fundamental connection, the relationship will not last.

The early days in a job are often described as a "honeymoon period." But any postwedding trip ends, and the newlyweds are faced with the practical realities of managing a life together. That's when the real work begins.

Consider the following trends from Hay Group's global employee opinion normative database. Figure 6.1 displays typical engagement and enablement index scores for employees with differing lengths of service with their current organizations. The trend lines display the U-shaped pattern commonly observed in most organizations.

Employees newest to the organization (those with less than one year of service) typically report the highest levels of motivation and support. Opinions tend to drop markedly among those with one to five years of service, before recovering somewhat for those with more than five years. Gains in employee opinion for long-tenured employees are likely due to both selection and adaptation. Those who are poor fits for the organization may exit to pursue options elsewhere, and those who remain long term are likely to be those who have found ways to adjust to the situations in which they find themselves.

Figure 6.1. Trends in engagement and enablement by tenure.

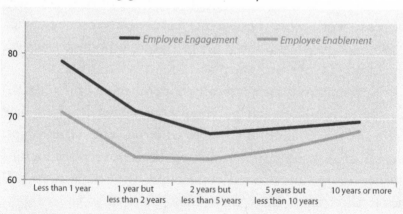

The common explanation for the tenure effect and for the subsequent declines in employees' satisfaction in the early years of employment with an organization is that the reality of the job is not what they were led to believe. In other words, the honeymoon is over.

Disillusionment or disengagement results from a lack of alignment between employees' expectations of the work and the reality they actually experience. For example, at Bernette, during the training period, no one mentioned to the new call center employees that in a matter of weeks they'd find out only at the last minute about new-product training sessions that might affect their work and personal schedules. And while they did hear about the Green Tree merger and how it would lead to more career opportunities as the bank grew, no one said anything about the current CRM integration issue and the problems it had created. For these inspired, optimistic new employees, a lack of enablement and subsequent frustration are almost certain to be right around the corner.

As with a new relationship, some of the tenure effect problems may stem from job applicants projecting their longings onto the organization, imagining that their new employer is the perfect match who will meet their every need. In other cases, new workers may be misled by an organization trying to "sell itself." Indeed, one client of ours joked that her organization rolls out the red carpet when interviewing prospective hires, but on the first day of work rolls out the linoleum!

Realistic Job Previews and Onboarding

In response, many organizations have looked to both prehire and posthire programs to help align new employees' expectations with organizational realities. These programs typically involve realistic job previews (RJPs) for prehires, and a more thorough onboarding experience for posthires.

RJPs provide candidates with straightforward, honest information about the positive and negative aspects of the job, the work environment, and the organization, "warts and all." While many applicants have limited understanding of the jobs for which they are applying, even greater percentages have no awareness whatsoever of the work environments they will be joining. Indeed, it is easier for prospective employees to understand how they will be paid in a new position and what they will be asked to do than it is for them to assess how it will feel to work in the organization. But the fit between the employee and the organization's work environment and operating style is one of the biggest factors in determining whether the employee will be productive and remain with the organization.

Industrial psychologists have researched the effects of RJPs. Their findings suggest that two "matchups" occur during the interview and hiring process: The employer matches its job requirements with the individual's qualifications, and the individual matches his or her needs with the company's culture and the job requirements. The first match has the greatest impact on performance, while the second has the largest effect on job satisfaction and, ultimately, retention.[1]

RJPs can be presented in a variety of media, including face-to-face presentations, videos, company tours, and written or electronic brochures. Depending on the job or the audience,

---

1. J. P. Wanous, "Organizational Entry: The Individual's Viewpoint," in *Perspectives on Behavior in Organizations*, 1st ed., ed. J. R. Hackman, E. Lawler, and L. Porter (New York: McGraw-Hill, 1977), 126–35.

some formats will be more successful than others. Some candidates or new employees will want to read about the job; others will prefer to hear about it; still others may gain the most understanding from a walk-through that exposes them to the actual work environment.

"Onboarding" is the process of acquiring, assimilating, and accelerating new users into an environment, culture, or methodology. It's much more than just a basic orientation. At work, as with personal relationships, you get only one chance to make a first impression. And advocates of employee onboarding like to stress the importance of making the most of a new hire's first ninety days to one year on the job, aka the "honeymoon."

Effective onboarding is critical to getting new employees off to a solid start in their roles and ensuring alignment with organizational cultures, expectations, and operating styles.

In today's world, where individuals move more frequently from organization to organization, onboarding new staff is a regular concern. And for organizations faced with rapid growth or high levels of turnover—such as call centers, hospitality companies, and retail operations—the challenges are particularly acute.

A human capital survey Hay Group recently conducted in partnership with the Society for Human Resource Management (SHRM) confirms that C-suite executives recognize the difficulties associated with bringing new people into the organization rapidly and effectively. Fully 70 percent of executives surveyed indicated that "onboarding and integrating new employees" is a moderate challenge, a significant challenge, or one of the biggest challenges facing their organizations at the present time.[2]

---

2. *Strategic Research on Human Capital Challenges: Final Report* (2007), SHRM Foundation.

Hay Group's employee opinion norms confirm that employees are similarly concerned about these issues. Roughly 45 percent of employees globally express neutral or unfavorable views of the job their organizations are currently doing in managing orientation programs and training new staff to do their jobs well.

Given that most organizations are running leaner and needing to get the most from all their people, getting new employees up to speed quickly is critical. Failing to do so can diminish productivity and place undue strains on existing staff.

Onboarding proponents believe that rather than delegating to coworkers the job of informally training newcomers (sometimes known as the "just follow him around" method of job orientation), or asking new hires to watch a video or read a brochure (typically on their own time), or simply throwing them in with the lions so they can learn by trial and error, responsibility for orienting new hires—and for managing their expectations about the reality of the job—should be a formal assignment within the organization. Sometimes, it can be valuable to have new employees, particularly those in leadership roles, start some onboarding activities even before their first day of work. There are many excellent Web-based learning modules to help kick-start the process in a way that's fun and engaging for new hires.

Enablement, Engagement, and the Tenure Effect

People typically enter an organization in an "effective" condition, displaying high levels of engagement and enablement. But over time, barriers to success faced by employees often have a negative effect in both areas.

Why doesn't a lack of enablement hit employees on day one? For one thing, expectations for individual contributions are typically modest when employees are new to their jobs and still "learning the ropes." To the extent that they are not expected to accomplish specific goals in their first weeks (or possibly even months), constraints don't yet bother them. Again, frustration involves the inability to achieve desired outcomes. If expectations for achievement are low in the early days of a role, frustration levels are likely to be low as well, even where enablement constraints are actually significant. One would have to work in the Bernette call center for a while, for example, before realizing how much time he or she is losing because of the lack of CRM system integration and effective communications. It won't feel like a lack of enablement at first.

Second (continuing with the romantic relationship metaphor), new employees struggling to get things done in the face of workplace constraints may conclude, "It's not you, it's me." That is, it can be hard for new employees to distinguish whether the problems they are facing stem from their own lack of experience and knowledge or instead the lack of an enabling environment.

But at some point employees get their sea legs. They understand their jobs, they understand the organization, and they begin to pursue goals. That's when a lack of enablement becomes a source of frustration. Notably, the *vision* employees have working for a company in advance of assuming a role in it is typically focused on engagement and its drivers. As with Bernette, employees are inspired to apply, to interview, and to accept a job offer from an organization because of its reputation, market position, future direction, and the career possibilities it offers. But the *reality* of working for the company is based more on enablement and its associated drivers. After the "honeymoon," the key issue is whether employees have what they need to get things done efficiently and effectively. As we've seen, for a growing number of Bernette employees the answer, lately at least, has been "no."

From there, as employees deal with their frustration, the typical responses discussed earlier surface. That's when some may begin problem solving to work around the lack of enablement. And that's when others may begin to withdraw, either by leaving the organization or by lowering their motivation levels and their willingness to expend discretionary effort.

So to yield better outcomes with new hires and sustain the positive outlook of new staff, should managers focus on engaging or enabling employees?

Prehire and posthire approaches (such as RJPs and onboarding activities) can, and certainly often do, help in properly aligning prospective/new employees' expectations with the reality of their jobs and the organization. But these approaches cannot alter the way work gets done, how the organization is structured, or how it is changing. New Bernette call center reps could be warned that the lack of CRM integration might negatively impact service levels. But those warnings would not do anything to reduce or solve the problems the new reps will soon face.

As a result, RJPs and onboarding can do little to ensure that employees are able to contribute to the organization in the most effective or optimal ways once they have been hired and acclimated. RJPs may help somewhat with the optimized roles component of enablement (increasing the fit between the individual and the job or organization). But, as with onboarding activities, they don't do anything to address the lack of support or barriers to performance that may be found in the work environment. RJPs and onboarding activities are meant to familiarize new employees with the organization as it *currently is*, rather than remedying any problems holding an organization back from what it *should be*. And if an organization is frustrating employees through constraints in the work environment, sensitizing employees to these constraints through RJPs or onboarding experiences will likely only serve to depress expectations and motivation, which, ironically enough, can hasten the disengagement or withdrawal process rather than preventing it.

Therefore, managing enablement levels, rather than expectations, is the more effective solution to the tenure effect. The key to sustaining the energy and positive outlook that new employees typically bring with them when they enter an organization is ensuring adequate support for success in job roles. Indeed, anytime leadership is looking at declining engagement levels, one of the first suspects should be a problem with enablement.

CHAPTER 7

Charting the Way Back on Track

BETH HADN'T SEEN Ray Pough since his send-off luncheon four months earlier. He'd left Bernette on good terms, still a great friend of the Ellsworth family and respected by employees at every level of the bank. Beth missed Bernette's former COO—missed working with him, missed his gentle humor and wit. Calm and steady, Ray had "grown up" at Bernette, having joined the bank fresh out of graduate school. As head of operations, he'd been instrumental in launching the online division and had worked closely with call center management on everything from workstation purchases, to IT, to policies. "I thought I'd be one of those dinosaurs who spend their entire careers in one place," Ray told Beth after they'd found a table at a coffee shop in downtown Denver. "It's so good to see you! How are things at Bernette?"

Ray must have seen something in Beth's eyes, because he held up one hand and answered his own question. "Good, but could be better, right?"

Beth smiled. "That's an excellent way to describe it, Ray," she said. He sipped his coffee as she continued. "It's still a great place. We're growing and the future looks bright. But some of us are a little concerned." She explained that while call center turnover was still far below industry average, it was creeping up. "I don't want to sound like I'm gossiping," she said, "it's just that I'd appreciate your insights here."

"What's going on?" Ray asked.

Beth described how the call center's CRM systems still hadn't been integrated and how training was nearly always scheduled at the last minute. "When a new product gets released, or when there's an update, we're the last to know," she said. "It costs a bundle in overtime. You know, with communications this slow, Lauren, Stacy, and I are always playing catch-up and putting out fires, so who has time to coach employees or go above and beyond?" She went on to explain that the call center was falling behind in maintaining service levels and how all these factors were beginning to weigh on her, on her colleagues, and on the reps. "Remember Bob the writer?" she asked.

"Sure," said Ray. "Good guy. Is he getting any more of his plays produced in town?"

"He's working on a collection of short stories," said Beth. Then she described Bob's dilemma to Ray.

"Bob will be okay," Ray told her. "He's been around for a long time, and this job is great for him because it gives him time to write and to be with his family. Sounds to me as though management is aware of the issue. He won't get fired, and eventually he'll make his way to marketing." He paused to take another sip of his steaming coffee. "But Beth," he added, "what about all the other Bobs whose issues haven't been identified? The high-potential people whose short-staffed managers refuse to promote. Or employees whose best strengths go unrecognized because there's no time for performance management.

Think of the untapped talent Bernette is sitting on. Bob's situation may be ironic, but the unidentified cases are downright tragic. It makes me wonder how many other people there could develop themselves by moving to another department if communication from department to department weren't stifled."

Beth nodded. Ray was probably right. Bob wasn't going to get fired. He was likely to grow more frustrated—and less productive—but eventually he'd be okay. The hurdles would be surmounted. But what about all the other missed opportunities?

"Why'd you leave Bernette, Ray?" Beth ventured.

Ray sat back and collected his thoughts for a moment. "Not to be too self-congratulatory," he said, "but I kind of felt this coming."

"Oh?" said Beth, somewhat surprised. She'd been told that he left to pursue new opportunities.

"It's not like I'm clairvoyant," said Ray. "At the time I couldn't articulate my concerns. But now that I have some distance from Bernette, I think I can see things a little more clearly." He paused for a moment to think about how to phrase what he was going to say next.

"You and the rest of the management team are putting out fires right now. But there are bigger issues, issues that you and Lauren might not have considered from your vantage point, but that need to be addressed," he began.

Beth nodded, appreciative of Ray's point of view. "Like what?" she asked.

"It's possible that what you see as a communications issue could be a symptom of something more fundamental. You mentioned scheduling reps. It could be that the problem lies in decision-making accountability, not just communications. If someone forgets to communicate, okay, that's not good, but it's a quick fix, right? 'Remember to tell the call center next time!' But perhaps the call center team shouldn't just be informed about what's happening and when, but also be involved in making those decisions, given the interdependencies between the call center and legal or marketing. Unless Bernette can think through and clarify those cross-functional relationships, energy and resources will continue to be wasted."

"So fixing the root problems is more than just buffing up the bank's communications," Beth observed.

"Right," said Ray. "It's not just a question of remembering to communicate. From a work structure and process perspective, it's important to step back and consider who should be making decisions. When a new regulation is released, reps of course need to be trained. But should legal have responsibility for determining the timing? Or should that decision be shared between legal and the call center? From an authority and empowerment perspective, it's important to define not only the decision responsibilities of functions but also which individuals will be given specific decision-making accountabilities. And from a collaboration perspective, appropriate mechanisms are needed to share the outcomes of decisions once they are made with the individuals and teams that will be affected by them."

"Ray, do you think Bernette can get back on track?" Beth asked.

"Yeah, actually, I do," he said. "How's your relationship with Angela Lohan?"

Beth winced. She described her talk with Angela, which, while ending cordially, didn't achieve the results Beth had been hoping for.

"Talk with her again," said Ray. "Maybe off-site, informally, but be very formal about what you present to her. You've got Lauren there, right?"

Beth nodded.

"Lauren and her forecasts are your trump card. She's the data queen. Ask her to make charts to show Angela how much the yearlong wait to integrate the CRMs is costing. There's your low-hanging fruit," he said. "It sounds to me like a pretty straightforward resource issue that can be resolved. I'd start there—don't throw a lot at Angela, just the CRM issue to start, and if that goes well, you could talk a little about overtime costs as well."

"I get it," said Beth. "Rome wasn't built in a day." She decided to talk with Lauren first thing in the morning. They'd make a plan and then approach Angela again.

"If anyone can get through to senior management, it's you two," said Ray. "The interesting thing is, there are no bad guys in this scenario. There are some newcomers there for sure, but to a large extent you've got a group of longtime employees who grew up together. It's like a family. And you know how it is with family—you sort of know what people are thinking. It's like that at Bernette. I think that's why there's resistance to formal processes. A lot of people there simply believe that processes aren't necessary because they never were before. But with all the growth you guys are dealing with, and all the growth you're hoping for, without some structure around decision making, training, and work processes, the place could really go downhill. You've outgrown informality, which is not a bad thing per se. A little structure around that stuff will make the place more efficient and enable people to perform better."

A week later, huddled in a booth at a local restaurant while waiting for Angela to arrive, Beth and Lauren did some last-minute planning. They wanted to keep their discussion with Angela positive. They wanted Angela to know that they were there to help, that they believed in the bank and wanted it to succeed. So they decided beforehand that instead of asserting anything to Angela, they would simply show her some data and ask how they could facilitate change and improvement. Their big hope was that Angela would listen with an open mind and not become defensive.

Nearly a year had elapsed since the merger, but the CRM systems were still not integrated. Reps who had to answer a Green Tree question from a Bernette CRM had to call a rep that happened to be on the right machine, or sometimes even leave their workstations and walk over to another rep's desk. How could that *not* affect service levels? So the plan was to make a logical case to Angela for the integration of the CRMs and better communications. Nothing was more important in the call center on a day-to-day basis.

Beth and Lauren had decided not to get into what had come to be known as "the Bob issue." That, they decided, could wait. If they could persuade Angela that the service levels would return as soon as the CRMs were integrated and that the bank would pay much less in overtime once some communications were formalized, those would be wins. And once Angela saw the results, wouldn't she be eager to listen to more of what Lauren and Beth had to say?

Lauren had come prepared with time sheets and call transcripts to demonstrate how much the lack of CRM integration was costing the bank. It wasn't simply a case of reps putting in a little more time to compensate for the CRM issues. Call center representatives were nonexempt from overtime rules. That meant if a rep worked more than forty hours a week, the rep was entitled to overtime under the law. Lauren knew it might be hard for Angela to appreciate someone showing up at 8:00, taking one hour's worth of breaks and a half-hour lunch, and walking out the door at 5:30 sharp. But Lauren was armed with time sheets to prove to Angela that every full-time rep was putting in a forty-hour week.

Angela was smart. There was no way she would dismiss Beth and Lauren and all their documentation in black and white. "No emotion, no defensiveness," Beth reminded Lauren a few minutes before Angela arrived. "She needs to come to the conclusion that what happens upstairs has an impact on the people. We shouldn't just tell her that people are frustrated. We need to tell her how much more we can do when we have the right tools at our disposal. Like Ray Pough suggested, let's keep this conversation strictly about the CRM issues and overtime. That's something the senior team can wrap their minds around. That's something we already know they intend to address. So let's show them a measure of our team's effectiveness before and after CRM integration. When Angela and her team make the connection between the state of our CRMs and the level of call center workers' frustration, they'll see the light!"

A minute later, Angela arrived. "So nice to see you outside of the office!" she said as she shook hands with both women. A waitress came by to take their drink orders—white wine for Beth and red for Angela, while Lauren splurged on a margarita. After drinks and small talk about family vacations and aging parents, Lauren cleared her throat, reached into her bag, and took out three time sheets and a small chart she had made based on Bernette's employee manual.

"Angela," Beth began, "Lauren put some documentation together. Really, I don't want to sound as though I'm being negative, but last time we spoke we didn't get off on the right foot. So . . ." Here she looked to Lauren. "This time—and really, thanks for taking the time to talk about this with us—this time we put together some charts to help provide a better picture of what our reps are up against."

The first chart showed a typical call center worker's out-of-adherence stats—bathroom breaks, meal breaks, even walks to the water cooler. Any time spent not at one's desk handling calls is considered out of adherence. "So, as you can see from this rep's call volume, she is at her desk taking calls for forty hours exactly on this week. And we have to keep in mind, these are all nonexempt jobs, so anything over forty hours and we have to pay overtime."

Angela studied the chart, then looked up at Beth. "You were right when you told me that everyone was working forty hours a week."

Beth smiled. "Like I told you that day in your office, we have reps working here twenty-four/seven. So any time you come in, you're going to see a few taking a break near the back door."

Angela did have to admit, after reviewing the charts, that every second of a call center worker's shift was accounted for. They were putting in forty hours a week at their stations, breaks or no. Whether a call center rep was on the phone, like most, or handling volumes of customer e-mail daily, like Bob, not only were these people busy, but their environment was stressful. Every call was monitored.

Next, Lauren showed Angela two transcripts of customer calls. In the first one, a one-page document, the customer asked about a new retirement savings program. The call was answered to the caller's satisfaction in less than one minute. "Now that's how a call should go," said Angela. "There's a rep who really knows her stuff."

Lauren nodded. "She's one of our best. Now, I'd like you to look at this second transcript. Lauren showed Angela a five-page document.

"Long call," said Angela, thumbing through the pages. "What did the customer want?"

"Well, that's the interesting part. The customer asked the exact same question about the exact same product. But as you can see, it took about seven minutes to complete the call. And by the end, the customer was not happy."

"What's the matter with that rep?" Angela snapped.

Lauren paused and then shared her surprise. "Actually, it's the same rep. During the first call she was on a Bernette CRM. She had all the answers at her fingertips. But the second transcript is from a different shift, and the rep had to sit at a different station. Unfortunately, her CRM was an old Green Tree system. So let's take a look at the transcript and see why the call took so long."

The transcript told the story. In a little less than the time it took for the rep to complete the first call, she searched the files in her system and realized that the product the customer was asking about wasn't there. That told the rep it wasn't a Green Tree product. The rep told the customer she was going to have to put him on hold. That on-hold lasted almost five minutes. That's because it took the rep more than three minutes to find another rep on a Bernette CRM who could look up the information. That rep had to put another customer on hold to field the first rep's call. "Now we have two customers on hold. Two calls that could have been resolved in just one minute each, but each one is taking several minutes."

Angela studied the charts, drew a deep breath, and whistled. "I had no idea," she said. "I thought that if they took fewer breaks . . ."

"We'd be paying overtime for that," said Beth.

"I see that now," said Angela. "And I can see why it is so difficult for the call center workers. We need to expedite CRM integration." Beth and Lauren glanced at each other. Success! Beth gestured to Lauren to continue.

"Now that we've got you interested, let me show you another chart." Lauren moved on to her next document. "This one shows overtime. We can see exactly how much overtime we're paying in the call center." The chart showed a total of $8,000 paid in overtime over a one-month period.

"That's high," said Angela.

"Couldn't agree more," said Lauren. "So let's look at chart number two here. For that month only $300 in overtime was paid to call center workers."

"How do we know this is an apples-to-apples comparison?" asked Angela.

"Glad you asked," said Lauren. "I chose these two months because of their similarities. Two times during each of these months I needed to schedule training sessions. One session was to introduce a new product, and the other session was on legal compliance. And just so we're on the same page, we had about the same number of overall employees during both of these months. Also, the training sessions were the same length."

"Then why did we pay so much more in overtime during this month?" Angela asked, pressing her finger into the offending chart, which lay on the table.

"Easy answer," said Lauren. "But you might not like it."

Angela waited expectantly.

Lauren pointed to the first chart, the one with $8,000 worth of overtime. "No one mentioned either of these trainings to me or to anyone else in the call center. I found out about them by chance, and I had only forty-eight hours to schedule the training. At the same time, I needed to fill seats in the call center. Because of the short notice, the only way we could get people in was by paying overtime."

Beth nodded to express her support, adding, "Angela, we don't know if this is just a simple lapse in communication or a symptom of something bigger, like a problem in our decision-making processes. But we wanted to show you how much it costs the bank when we don't hear about a need for training until the last minute."

Lauren showed Angela the second chart. "This one's a little over a year old," she said. "This is before the merger. I had a one-month heads-up before the trainings so we had plenty of time to schedule them. It was no problem reworking the master schedule so we could fill seats at the call center and the training center, and hardly pay any overtime."

It was time for Beth to take over. She thanked Lauren for making the charts and sharing them with Angela. "As you can see," Beth told Angela, "when our reps have the tools and resources they need—like the right CRMs with the right products loaded in—they can do their jobs better. It's not about taking fewer breaks. It's about efficiency."

Lauren and Beth could see it in Angela's eyes. They'd gotten through to her. She finally understood something about some of the barriers in the call center and how much it might be costing the bank. Lauren and Beth were right. If the senior team were to enable the call center workers, supervisors, and managers, it would go directly to Bernette's bottom line: less paid in overtime, more satisfied customers, and longer tenure for employees.

Angela stood up to leave. "This has been a revelation," she told Beth and Lauren. "I want you to know that you have my full support. You went out of your way to prove something to me. So first thing tomorrow I will have a talk with Howard. He needs to buy in to this. And I know he will. I have to approach him as thoughtfully as you approached me. In fact, Lauren, will you join me with Howard? You can do a better job stepping him through your charts than I can."

"I'd be happy to talk to Howard with you," said Lauren. "I'll show him the charts. We'll get him on the same page as us, and we can turn things around!"

The next day, in a reception area across town, Stacy sat patiently reading some materials about the new bank where she was interviewing. Everyone seemed nice. She had never actually interviewed for an executive position before. But she'd have her MBA in a few months. She'd won some awards in graduate school, even while working full-time and taking classes at night. Stacy had made a good impression during her first interview. When asked why she was planning to leave her longtime employer, she had had her answer down pat. Not only did she want to expand her experience base, but also at this bank (which, like Bernette, was growing through acquisition) operations were a real focus.

Of course Stacy knew not to trash-talk her current employer. So she had put a warm spin on the problems she faced in the call center. And in fact, she wasn't even angry that the integration was taking longer than it should or that communications were slow and sometimes nonexistent. Anger wasn't the right word. Frustration. That's what had set in.

"Stacy Robbins?" An administrative assistant ushered Stacy through a network of hallways into the bright-white office of the bank's senior vice president of finance. Stacy had a good feeling in this new place. She'd heard that attrition was very low, so they must be doing something right. The people she saw in the halls and at their desks looked happy. But really, what did that tell her? Not much. She'd have a few questions of her own to ask the VP. And the VP seemed pleased that Stacy had come prepared.

The VP was a middle-aged man named Peter Michaels. He too had worked his way up from a call center. Right from the get-go, they had something in common. After a few questions and a more in-depth discussion of salary and bonuses, the interview drifted into sharing call center stories. This guy Peter really got it! He was finance, not operations, but he knew more about call centers than Angela did.

Stacy's second interview went well. At the end she stood up, shook hands with Peter, and thanked him for his time. "I learned a lot, and I'm excited about the opportunity to come work for you," she told him.

Peter shook Stacy's hand, looked her in the eye, and promised she'd be hearing from him soon. He thought to himself that she reminded him of a younger version of himself: about to be a newly minted MBA, plenty of experience in a call center, and a great attitude. He decided that after checking her references, if there were no red flags, he would make her an offer.

After congratulating himself on finding such a good new assistant director of finance, he thought about what the competition was about to lose. He knew Bernette's reputation in the industry. He knew its good name throughout Denver and that people across the country did their banking with Bernette-Online because it offered reliable, affordable, easy-to-use services. And he knew Howard Ellsworth. It was only a matter of time before Howard realized there was a problem and turned things around.

Peter smiled to himself. He wondered how long the window would stay open, how long he could poach frustrated employees from Bernette. Even if he had just a month, he figured he could hire away a manager or two, and maybe his bank's call center could pick up a few folks from Bernette's. Hiring away from Bernette was great, he thought. The call center workers had already been vetted. They'd already been trained. Getting them up to speed on a new—and integrated—CRM was a piece of cake. Bernette call center people were the best in the business. That bank had won so many awards in the past. They knew how to work with customers. With frustration running so high at Bernette, Peter could safely assume that Stacy would not be the last Bernette employee to come looking for a job with the competition. Bernette's loss was his bank's gain.

⌒

The day after the big meeting with Angela, Lauren and Beth decided to go out for lunch and have a small celebration. Lauren went to find Stacy to invite her to join them and give her the good news. But Stacy wasn't at her desk or anywhere to be found on the floor.

"Anyone seen Stacy?" Lauren called out to no one in particular.

The answer came from a rep in a cubicle three rows down from where Lauren stood. He tugged at his earpiece to free his mouth and called out, "Stacy had a doctor's appointment. Said she'd be back after lunch."

Lauren didn't want to say what she was thinking. Maybe Stacy actually did have a doctor's appointment. Then again, that morning Stacy had seemed pretty well-dressed. The call center was business casual, but Stacy had shown up in a smart gray business suit.

Lauren hoped against hope. Who knows? Maybe Stacy was the type of person who dressed up for doctor's appointments.

Beth came up behind Lauren, took her by the arm, and began leading her out the door. "Did you find Stacy? Is she coming?"

Even as Lauren said "doctor's appointment," it sounded like code for "job interview." Until recently she had been job hunting herself, as Beth knew.

"Stacy will be thrilled," Beth said as the two of them left the building and headed across the parking lot. It was a gorgeous spring day. No jackets required. The sun had warmed Beth's car. The two women sat side by side, feeling reenergized, feeling optimistic, knowing that a big, welcome change was about to come. They pulled out of the lot, drove south on Broadway for a few blocks, and then stopped at a red light. They sat in silence for a moment. Then something occurred to Beth. She turned to Lauren. "A doctor's appointment?" she asked. "In *those* heels?"

CHAPTER 8

Understanding Enablement

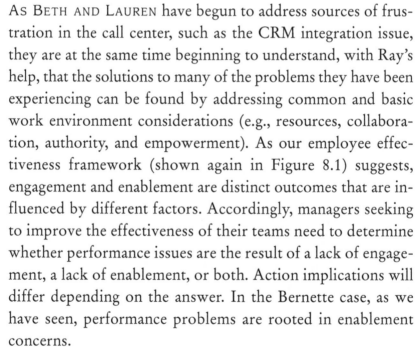

As Beth and Lauren have begun to address sources of frustration in the call center, such as the CRM integration issue, they are at the same time beginning to understand, with Ray's help, that the solutions to many of the problems they have been experiencing can be found by addressing common and basic work environment considerations (e.g., resources, collaboration, authority, and empowerment). As our employee effectiveness framework (shown again in Figure 8.1) suggests, engagement and enablement are distinct outcomes that are influenced by different factors. Accordingly, managers seeking to improve the effectiveness of their teams need to determine whether performance issues are the result of a lack of engagement, a lack of enablement, or both. Action implications will differ depending on the answer. In the Bernette case, as we have seen, performance problems are rooted in enablement concerns.

In this chapter, we briefly review the determinants of employee engagement before turning to the key work environment factors that managers, such as those at Bernette, need to

Figure 8.1. Employee effectiveness framework.

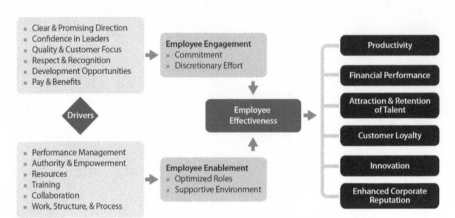

monitor and manage to ensure that motivated employees are well-positioned to succeed.

What Drives Engagement?

As our framework indicates, fostering high levels of employee engagement involves two key concerns:

1. Building employees' confidence in the future of the organization (through Clear & Promising Direction, Confidence in Leaders, Quality & Customer Focus) as well as employees' roles in it (i.e., Development Opportunities)

2. Ensuring that employees are adequately rewarded for their contributions to company success (through Pay & Benefits and Respect & Recognition)

Clarifying the practical implications of organizational directions is, of course, essential to effective execution. But connecting employees with the big picture is equally important from a motivational perspective. In their work, most employees are looking for an opportunity to contribute to something larger than themselves, a chance to make a difference. Appealing to this sense of purpose is the essence of transformational leadership and critical to promoting high levels of employee engagement. At Bernette Financial, for example, serving the community is part of the bank's mission. The message is embraced by—and communicated from—senior management to middle management straight to the hourly employees working in the call center.

Ensuring that employees have confidence that there are strong hands on the wheel that are capable of executing on strategic objectives is also critical for engagement. Today's employees recognize that their prospects for continued employment and career development are dependent on their companies' health, stability, and future direction. They know that playing for a winner is more important than ever. Employees cannot be expected to bind their futures to those of their employers unless they are confident that their companies are well-managed and positioned for success.

Demonstrating to employees that the organization is focused on its customers, delivers high-quality products and services, and is innovative in developing new offerings is likewise essential for building employee confidence in the direction and future market position of the organization. And for any employees in customer-facing roles (like the call center team at Bernette), nothing dissatisfies them faster than the sense that the organization doesn't "get it" or seemingly doesn't care when it comes to what customers require. After all, these employees are on the front lines in dealing with customers, and they are direct recipients of any negative customer feedback.

Because the social contract surrounding the employment relationship has been redefined, and the old loyalty-for-security bargain has been cast aside, employees are increasingly aware that they are responsible for managing and developing their own careers and that their futures depend on continuous elevation of their skills. If they are not expanding their capabilities, they risk compromising their employability, within their current organizations or elsewhere. Accordingly, opportunities for growth and development are among the most consistent predictors of employee engagement.

With today's organizations operating increasingly lean, employees are being asked to do more with less. In high-workload environments especially, employees are sensitized to compensation issues. Acutely aware of all they are contributing, they are inclined to pressure their organizations to balance rewards and contributions. In this context, it is more important than ever that compensation systems be perceived to reward employee efforts adequately. Clarifying the equity of pay systems both internally and externally is critical to building employees' confidence that they are receiving an appropriate return on their investments in the organization.

Numerous studies have suggested, however, that nonmonetary rewards and recognition are often more effective motivators than money. It's not that money doesn't matter. It's just that money tends to be a "deficiency need." If employees feel that they are significantly underpaid—that their pay does not reflect their contributions to the organization—their motivation is likely to suffer. But when it comes to encouraging employees to pour discretionary effort into their work and deliver superior performance, the chance to make a difference and be recognized for it is likely to provide a much stronger incentive. As Harvard Business School professor Rosabeth Moss Kanter puts it: "Compensation is a right. Recognition is a gift." The fact that patting employees' backs may be a more effective form of positive motivation than padding their wallets is good news for companies, especially when compensation budgets are stretched to the limit. Unlike compensation, recognition is inexpensive. Indeed, often it's free.

Positioning Motivated Employees to Succeed

Our research confirms that many organizations that have enviably high levels of employee engagement still struggle with performance issues. So while necessary, engagement alone is not sufficient for achieving maximum levels of individual and organizational performance. Leaders and managers must not only engage and motivate employees but also enable them to direct their extra efforts productively and effectively. Think about Bernette. Employees there are, by anyone's standards, engaged. But are they equipped? Are they enabled?

As we have discussed, leaders and managers at different levels in the organization may have differing abilities to impact the drivers of employee engagement and employee enablement. Strategic issues of the sort that affect engagement may be most appropriately addressed by senior executives, while operational factors impacting employee enablement may be more directly under the control of local management and first-line supervisors. By better focusing managers on the issues that they can and should be addressing—and demonstrating the connection between these issues and individual, work group, and organizational effectiveness—our model facilitates action planning that will more likely lead to sustainable organizational improvement.

Enhancing Employee Enablement

Employee enablement involves getting people in job roles that draw on their distinctive abilities to contribute, as well as ensuring that they are able to carry out their job responsibilities as efficiently and effectively as possible. In the following section, we highlight factors that promote both high levels of role optimization and a supportive work environment.

Performance Management

Key considerations:
- ► Specify clearly what employees need to accomplish.
- ► Set challenging but attainable performance standards.
- ► Provide ongoing feedback regarding progress relative to goals.

Regular conversations about employee performance are critical to ensuring that motivated employees are well-positioned to succeed. First, managers need to specify for employees which personal goals and priorities are the most critical, especially in high-workload environments. Doing so allows employees to focus their efforts on essential, value-added tasks (the "must-win battles") in cases where there is too much to do and too little time to do it. Second, regular discussions about employee performance can help root out barriers to success that may exist in the work environment, allowing managers and employees to take timely corrective action. Finally, by continually "raising the bar," ongoing monitoring and feedback on performance helps ensure that role definitions and role assignments allow employee capabilities to be developed and used to their full potential.

Effectively managing employee performance requires that organizations treat performance appraisals not as discrete one-time events, but instead as a continual dialogue between an employee and his or her supervisor. Unfortunately, the reality is often far from the ideal. In many organizations, managers and employees alike dread performance appraisals and see them as a necessary evil inflicted on them by the HR department. Occurring only a few days per year, they result in little meaningful feedback. One manager noted that annual performance reviews "are like delivering a newspaper to a house with a growling dog. You throw the paper on the porch and get away as quickly as possible."[1] Ironically, with the right kind of performance-based dialogue, managers could eliminate the annual performance review altogether. In a true culture of dialogue, feedback is given consistently in small doses, and the annual review becomes a nonevent.

---

1. "Managing Performance: Achieving Outstanding Performance Through a Culture of Dialogue," Hay Group White Paper, 2002.

Authority & Empowerment

Key considerations:

► Give employees the authority and decision-making responsibility needed to do their jobs.

► Allow employees to have input into the way their work is structured.

► Encourage employees to come up with new and better ways of doing things.

A critical component of employee enablement is "role optimization." In deploying talent, managers need to consider not only the requirements of the job and an employee's ability to meet them, but also the extent to which the job will draw on and leverage the employee's distinctive competencies. Where employees have appropriate autonomy and discretion, they are better able to structure their work arrangements to promote personal effectiveness. And by managing how they work, employees are more likely to find opportunities to leverage their skills and abilities fully in their job roles.

Hay Group's approach to designing jobs takes into account the size and shape of the job, that is, the skills, experience, problem solving, and decision making required. If a job is assigned too much accountability, people in the role will be short of skills and experience, and easily overwhelmed. Conversely, if too little accountability is assigned, incumbents will be bored and the organization will spend too much and get too little in return.

Well-designed jobs have explicit decision-making authority, and this authority must be commensurate with accountabilities. Without the appropriate decision-making authority, people cannot, or will not, act as required by their jobs. Clearly defining and bounding the decision rights associated with job roles might at first glance be interpreted as placing constraints on innovation and limiting empowerment. However, our research on effective organizations shows quite the opposite. Empowerment requires "specific freedom to act." When the scope of decision making is unclear or managers and employees receive mixed messages, they will be inclined not to take risks or make even simple decisions.

Where organizations face challenging economic environments or strong competitive pressures, it is essential that they take full advantage of any and all opportunities to root out inefficiencies (i.e., gaps and overlaps) in job roles and work processes. While effective job and organization design is part of the solution, so too is harnessing the creative ideas of employees at all levels. To draw out improvement suggestions broadly, organizations need to ensure that leaders and cultural cues encourage employees to come forward with innovative suggestions for improving the way work is done and reinforce the value of employee creativity by appropriately translating ideas into action.

Resources

Key considerations:

► Give employees the resources they need to do their jobs.

► Ensure all information needed is readily available and up-to-date.

► Maintain adequate staffing levels and review job designs and workloads when the organization changes.

Providing engaged employees with resources sufficient to carry out their jobs is critical to leveraging their energy. Resourcing employees appropriately to perform effectively involves more than budget considerations. Along with adequate financial support, employees require adequate tools, equipment, and supplies. And, especially in rapidly changing environments, organizations need to ensure that employees have the information they need to carry out their roles in ways that align with broader organizational goals and objectives.

For lean organizations, staffing levels are a continual concern. Faced with challenging economic environments and competitive pressures, many organizations have reduced headcounts without corresponding reduction in the amount of work to be done, resulting in higher workloads for remaining employees. Often at the same time compensation budgets are being squeezed. As they are striving to do more with less, organizations need to ensure sufficient staffing in different work areas to avoid employee burnout and to maintain high levels of product and service quality.

Even in cases where budget constraints won't allow hiring additional employees, there are still steps that can be taken to address staffing concerns. Managers should, for instance, work closely with HR to ensure that vacancies created by turnover are filled as quickly as possible. Likewise, through careful scheduling of work and thoughtful use of temporary/contract employees, managers can minimize the workflow disruptions associated with employee vacations or absences. Finally, managers should consider performance levels and the alignment of people with roles. When staffing levels are tight, managers cannot afford to have individuals failing to meet expectations or failing to leverage their full capabilities.

Training

> Key considerations:
>
> ▶ Get new employees fully trained before expecting full performance.
>
> ▶ Ensure skills of current employees keep up with changing job demands.
>
> ▶ Provide opportunities for employees to expand their current skill sets.

In a supportive environment, new and existing employees are provided with job-related training to ensure they have the knowledge and skills necessary to carry out key tasks and deal effectively with internal and external customers. Appropriate training, which can turn potential into productivity, is essential to ensure that organizations get the most from the abilities of their employees. Often, when financial resources are strained, organizations are forced to make cuts in training budgets. In doing so, however, leaders are wise to identify and protect high-value training offerings and training that is focused on high-potential employees.

Hay Group's employee opinion surveys suggest that most employees have favorable opinions of the training opportunities their organizations offer to assist them with continued learning and development. Despite the availability of training, however, *access* to these offerings remains an issue. Nearly one-third report that they are generally too weighed down by day-to-day job responsibilities to take advantage of job-related training.

Money spent on developing training programs is money wasted if employees aren't freed up to attend. And over the long term, a continued focus on developing employees is essential to ensuring that talent needs are met. Demographic trends, including declining birth rates in many Western countries and the looming exit of the post–World War II "baby boom" generation from the workforce, signal that competition for talent is likely to continue well into the future.

Collaboration

> Key considerations:
>
> ▶ Facilitate strong cooperation and teamwork within the unit.
> ▶ Establish supportive relationships with other groups to which the unit is connected.
> ▶ Promote effective sharing of resources and information across the organization.

Effective working relationships within and across departments support employees in delivering their best work and providing high levels of customer service. Sharing information and resources also promotes innovation, which can contribute not only to new products and services but also to better and more efficient ways of working.

Hay Group employee surveys confirm that most organizations today are struggling to establish effective collaboration and teamwork across departments. Nearly one-quarter of respondents indicate that teamwork between departments in their organizations is inadequate, and more than one-third of respondents report that communication between departments is insufficient.

In his book *Who Says Elephants Can't Dance?* describing his experiences in turning IBM around, Lou Gerstner notes that "one of the most surprising (and depressing) things I have learned about large organizations is the extent to which individual parts of an enterprise behave in an unsupportive and competitive way toward other parts of the organization. . . . Individuals and departments jealously protect their prerogatives, their autonomy, their turf."[2] Especially in challenging economic environments, managers and employees may be inclined to hunker down and focus on the achievement of individual or departmental priorities. It is critical that organizational cultures, performance management systems, and hiring and promotion processes reinforce the need for managers and employees to "wear their enterprise hats" and balance local concerns with broader organizational needs.

Work, Structure, & Process

Key considerations:

► Structure and organize work processes within your unit to ensure optimal efficiency.

2. L. Gerstner, *Who Says Elephants Can't Dance? Inside IBM's Historic Turnaround* (New York: HarperCollins, 2002).

> ► Coordinate with other units to clarify decision-making accountabilities and enhance cross-unit operating effectiveness.
>
> ► Continually seek new technologies and creative approaches to improve overall internal effectiveness.

Collaboration as well as Work, Structure, & Process are concerned with the interconnections that exist within an organization. Collaboration deals with the interpersonal side of work relationships, whereas Work, Structure, & Process relates to the formal systems and decision-making structures that support interdependencies both within and across units.

From a productivity perspective, organizations operating in increasingly competitive environments can ill afford to squander resources and employee effort through suboptimal processes. But efficient operations are equally important to sustaining high levels of employee motivation. Where employees are being asked to work hard, they understandably want to feel that they are working "smart" as well. At a minimal level, employees need to feel that the organization is not introducing barriers to getting their jobs done. And, ideally, they should have the sense that the organization is doing all it can to promote their success.

Given that time available for work is finite and work demands are unlikely to decrease anytime soon, fostering supportive work environments is also critical for helping employees achieve reasonable work-life balance. As we discussed in Chapter 4, long-term solutions to work-life balance concerns need to focus on helping employees work more productively. Organizations with enabling environments limit the extent to which work tasks "crowd out" personal time by permitting employees to complete the most vital tasks as efficiently as possible. Even when workloads are heavy, employees are likely to feel far better about staying late or coming in early if they feel that work is well-organized and carried out as efficiently as possible.

To maintain high levels of operating efficiency over time, organizations need to reexamine existing processes continually to identify opportunities for improvement that leverage new technologies and the innovative ideas of employees at all levels. Operational excellence involves proactively addressing potential problems before they occur and providing support for innovation even in areas of current strength.

▷ Deeper Dive: Enablement and Market Differentiation

In their book *The Discipline of Market Leaders*, Michael Treacy and Fred Wiersema argue that the best companies succeed by focusing on one of three value disciplines.[3] Some choose to compete on *operational excellence* and emphasize efficient delivery of products and services at the lowest possible cost. Others strive for *product leadership* and seek to establish a market position based on the innovativeness of their offerings. And still others aim to succeed by creating *customer intimacy* through exceptional levels of service and responsiveness. Notably, enablement concerns are fundamental to each of these competitive approaches.

---

3. M. Treacy and F. Wiersema, *The Discipline of Market Leaders: Choose Your Customers, Narrow Your Focus, and Dominate Your Market* (New York: Perseus Books, 1995).

Operational Excellence

For companies seeking to compete on operational excellence, smooth operations are absolutely essential. That puts emphasis, of course, on work, structure, and process efficiencies. Consider an example from Walmart, the company founded on Sam Walton's "always low prices" philosophy. Walmart recently began contacting suppliers to its four thousand U.S. stores with a request to take over deliveries of suppliers' products in cases where Walmart can manage the logistics for less, and use the savings to reduce the prices customers face.[4]

Promoting high levels of authority and empowerment is important to allow employees to contribute ideas for rooting out performance obstacles and finding new and better ways of doing things. Consider another example, from a recent *Bloomberg BusinessWeek* story on the margin-pressured food business. On a daily basis, workers at the Campbell Soup factory in Maxton, North Carolina, gather prior to the start of their shifts to identify opportunities to save the company time, money, and effort. Their suggestions have resulted in significant improvements in productivity. On a broth line at the plant that processes more than 260 million pounds of ingredients a year, for example, "operators and mechanics numbered each gasket to speed repairs. They cut windows into the metal coverings of conveyor belts so they can spot the signs of wear. They color-coded valve handles to avoid confusion in settings."[5] The end result? Operating efficiency has risen to 85 percent of levels managers regard as maximum targets, a ten-percentage-point gain over a three-year period.

4. "Why Wal-Mart Wants to Take the Driver's Seat," *Bloomberg BusinessWeek*, May 27, 2010.

5. "Campbell's Quest for Productivity," *Bloomberg BusinessWeek*, November 24, 2010.

Product Leadership

Our research with Most Admired Companies that are particularly well-regarded for innovativeness (i.e., innovation leaders) confirms that authority and empowerment and collaboration are critical to developing new ideas and leveraging existing ones. As with biological evolution, organizational innovation is fueled by experimentation. Most Admired Companies tend to recruit more than their fair share of the best and the brightest talent. And our research has consistently shown that they leverage the skills and capabilities of their people by giving them broad latitude in carrying out their job responsibilities. Recognizing that pursuing innovative ideas often requires people to go beyond the formal limits of their responsibility, innovation leaders foster high levels of empowerment. They ensure that decisions are made at the right level (i.e., where the most appropriate knowledge and expertise reside). And they encourage managers and employees to take reasonable risks in an attempt to increase organizational effectiveness.

By definition, of course, risk taking involves the potential for failure as well as success. And organizations can quickly kill entrepreneurial spirit if people know they will be punished for every promising idea that doesn't work out in the end. Innovation leaders discourage people from "playing it safe" by creating climates where innovative ideas can fail without penalty to the originating person or group.

While creativity is an essential ingredient in innovation, new approaches don't only result from new ideas. "Old" ideas may also serve as the raw material for new ideas, if recombined in productive ways through effective collaboration. Indeed, John W. Leikhim, Procter & Gamble's former director of corporate R&D, argues that the ability to leverage existing knowledge is a critical component of P&G's innovation success. "Our hidden secret," he notes, "is that P&G has significant continuity in developing a critical mass of knowledge. We work in five industry groups. And by having people in these industry groups, we have an incredible ability to cross-fertilize our know-how and to make connections that create real synergies and opportunities to develop new markets in our existing businesses. This 'web of interconnectivity' has been a powerful engine of growth for P&G." To develop the highly successful Crest White Strips teeth-whitening system, for example, P&G drew on substrate technology developed in the family care business and research on hydrogen peroxide bleaching being conducted by the laundry business. When these ideas were combined by the oral care business, a new product was born.

Cross-functional teams are commonly employed as a mechanism for developing innovative ideas. And the use of such teams does not distinguish innovation leaders from other companies. Innovation leaders are distinctive, however, in encouraging higher levels of spontaneous, informal cooperation and collaboration. They are more likely to report that they do a good job of capturing ideas and best practices and diffusing them throughout the organization. P&G, for example, maintains communities of practice that span different business units and form a "virtual organization" for this purpose.

Customer Intimacy

If employees are to deliver high levels of customer service, it is essential that organizations establish the appropriate foundation. Hay Group has conducted extensive research linking employee and customer survey data to identify the factors in the work environment that are most predictive of the quality of customer experiences. Our findings consistently point to authority and empowerment and collaboration as key considerations for fostering high levels of customer loyalty.

Empowering front-line, customer-facing employees is fundamental to the approaches of organizations that are recognized as customer loyalty leaders. After all, a customer with a question or problem wants a quick response and isn't likely to be happy if he or she has to wait for an employee to consult a manual or a supervisor before providing an answer or a resolution. Whether it is urban legend or not, Nordstrom customers often tell a story of an individual who came into a store one day wanting to return a set of snow tires. Of course, Nordstrom doesn't sell snow tires and never has. But knowing that satisfying valued customers is the overriding goal, the sales associate was empowered to make the decision to accept the return in the interest of making a customer happy.

Collaboration is likewise essential for creating positive customer experiences. It stands to reason that if employees are working together well and supporting each other internally, they will be better able to serve customers externally. To illustrate the importance of the internal customer service chain, Richard Branson, founder of the Virgin Group, tells the story of a customer whose free Virgin Atlantic Upper Class limo failed to pick him up at his hotel, forcing him to catch a cab to the airport in heavy traffic. When he arrived at the airport, late and angry, the Virgin agent who met him refunded his cab fare out of her own pocket and rushed him to the gate in time for his flight. Unfortunately, however, her supervisor refused to reimburse her for the $70 outlay because she had failed to get a receipt. "One thing was certain," Branson notes. "Any Virgin employees witnessing their supervisor's scornful reaction to their colleague's exemplary deed would be unlikely to display the same resourcefulness. Which means that the customer loses and so does the entire company."[6]

6. Richard Branson, "Richard Branson on Customer Service," *Entrepreneur*, January 10, 2011.

Ritz Carlton, famous for its high levels of service to hotel guests, is another example of the importance of enabling employees to promote positive customer experiences. The service values that are imparted to employees emphasize both individual initiative and collaborative support among colleagues. Among the twelve core values: "I am empowered to create unique, memorable and personal experiences for our guests," "I own and immediately resolve guest problems," and "I create a work environment of teamwork and lateral service so that the needs of our guests and each other are met."

In the next chapters, we'll see how Bernette Financial begins to tackle its enablement issues through effective performance management, by empowering managers and employees, by ensuring adequate resources and training, by aligning work, structure and processes, and by ensuring a collaborative environment. While the work involved is not easy, it's not rocket science either. In fact, we have seen it take place in organizations of all sizes, and across all industries.

CHAPTER 9

Tackling Bernette's Enablement Issues

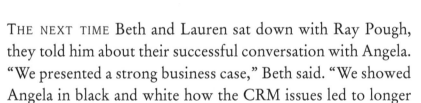

THE NEXT TIME Beth and Lauren sat down with Ray Pough, they told him about their successful conversation with Angela. "We presented a strong business case," Beth said. "We showed Angela in black and white how the CRM issues led to longer calls and lower service levels. Now, at the very least, we have the issue on her radar screen."

Ray added that the talk Beth and Lauren had with Angela would likely go a long way toward Beth's getting a seat at the table with senior management, so that "eventually, when Howard sits down with his heads of marketing, finance, operations, and legal, and he hears what's happening in those areas, he'll hear what's happening in the call center too."

Lauren felt that part of their success to date lay in the fact that they hadn't addressed multiple issues in their one sitting with Angela. "We stuck to call time and work-around time, and we didn't make an emotional plea. We didn't tell Angela that the call center employees were frustrated or unhappy."

"Sounds like a win," said Ray.

Both women agreed.

"Of course there's still much to be done," Ray explained. "The good news is that you two can accomplish a lot to address employee frustration even without senior management's formal buy-in. It sounds to me as though there are things you can begin right now."

Beth and Lauren were happy to hear this. "A lot of enablement solutions are pretty basic," Ray continued. "I recommend talking with every employee on your team, asking them specifically what frustrates them, and listening to their ideas. This may take some time, but I can practically guarantee you that you'll hear amazing things from your people."

"We'll have those talks," Beth said. "But what can we do to improve communication across departments? Like I told you, the development team will work with marketing to create a new product. But by the time anyone at the call center hears about it, it's about to launch, and our people have had no training in it, so they can't upsell it to callers."

Ray thought for a moment. Then he asked Lauren and Beth, "Why do you think the senior-level managers don't share information? Sometimes when that happens, it's because managers are afraid of losing control. It's political. It's about power. You know?"

"Yes," said Beth. "I know what you're talking about, but I don't think that's the case at Bernette. Lauren?"

Lauren agreed. "I think Bernette people are sincere," she said. "They want to get the word out about new products. It's just that we never really had a method of doing that before. When the bank was smaller, when a new product came out, everyone knew. I think it's more a case of having outgrown the old way without thinking through a new way."

"Fair enough," said Ray. "So let me ask you this: Putting

new products aside for a moment, are cross-functional teams used to promote interaction and sharing of information across the whole bank?"

Beth and Lauren shook their heads in unison. "No way," said Lauren.

"No regular opportunities for employees to interact with people from other teams?" Ray asked.

"Not really," said Beth. "People still communicate informally. I think that's part of the problem."

"Exactly," said Ray. "In a growing organization, informal systems will often break down and need to be replaced with more formal processes. Why don't we start thinking about ways to make sure the interactions happen?"

Lauren had an idea. "There is a monthly marketing staff meeting that could provide a good opportunity to share information between the call center and marketing," she said, looking at Beth. "Maybe someone from the call center should attend regularly. We could do that without even running it by senior management. I seriously doubt that anyone in marketing would mind."

"Sounds like a good idea," said Ray. "If I were you, first thing in the morning tomorrow, I'd talk with my marketing colleagues about joining that meeting."

Lauren and Beth thanked Ray for his advice. They decided to talk with every call center rep to learn what was at the root of the reps' frustration. And they'd get on board for that monthly marketing meeting, too. Then, armed with plenty of hard data and anecdotal reports, they'd have another talk with the senior team.

As they were getting ready to leave, Lauren asked Ray the same thing Beth had asked at their last meeting: "What have you been doing since you left the bank?" It had become something of a mystery. To the best of everyone's knowledge, Ray was no longer working in banking or financial services.

Ray smiled demurely. "Keeping busy with a few pet projects," he said. Lauren waited for more, but Ray wasn't forthcoming. She didn't want to push. After all, Ray was such a help to her and Beth. But she was curious about where he was working. Was he in a whole new industry? Starting up a new business? Whatever it was, he wasn't talking.

≁

Over the next few days, Beth and Lauren met with each and every call center employee to talk about enablement. Because people had to be on duty at all times, they met with small groups at every shift. There were no shortcuts. All the conversations were face-to-face. "We're going to talk a lot about frustration during this session, and I want to hear from you." That's how Beth opened every discussion. "Our turnover is still pretty low, and we want to keep it that way. We don't want to lose good people. And if you are here today, please know that we value you. You were hired because we believe in you. But we realize that belief isn't enough. So we're here to enable you so that you can do your best work here."

The meetings were followed up by e-mails from Beth that gave everyone a chance to communicate. "Some people might feel uncomfortable speaking up in a group setting," Beth reasoned. "Different people have different communication preferences, and I want to hear from everyone who has something to say." Beth included her direct line phone number in each e-mail. "If you want to talk about this, please call me," she wrote.

In addition to the in-person talks, Lauren posted a blog on

Bernette's intranet and sent everyone a link to it, inviting them to read it and reply. A lively online discussion ensued. When encouraged to do so, call center employees were willing to talk about what frustrated them and how that frustration might be relieved.

After the first couple of meetings, Beth and Lauren sat down to compare notes. Both were amazed by what they'd heard. Time after time, reps from different shifts who didn't even know one another told eerily similar tales of how they nearly quit when they were not able to provide customers with accurate and timely answers to their questions. More than one told of customers who had threatened to withdraw all their money from Bernette and put it into accounts at other banks. And a few customers had actually done it! Lauren decided to begin tracking that statistic, and taking a closer look at the periodic customer satisfaction surveys that some callers received after their issues were resolved. After all, she wanted a baseline against which to measure progress under the new strategy. These data could come in handy when she or Beth next talked with senior management.

Reflecting on her conversation with Ray, Beth sat at her desk and thought about his advice. Ray was right: There was a lot she and Lauren could do even without senior management's buy-in, like addressing the call center's "average handle time" for example.

One of the comments heard most often from Bernette call center representatives was that while things on the ground were changing (new products, new bank rules, new legislation affecting banking), no one seemed to recognize that the reps required time to adjust. Management's expectations never seemed to change.

At a typical call center, average handle time (AHT) equals:

- ▶ "Agent talk time" (time spent talking/listening to customers) plus

- ▶ "Hold time" (how long customers are placed on hold) plus

- ▶ "After call work time" (time spent after customer has hung up to enter a work order).

Of course, call centers want shorter AHT. After all, time is money. When an agent has a new process, policy, or product to learn, typically AHT goes up because of the rep's learning curve.

In the old days at Bernette, an increase in AHT would spark an informal investigation. Someone would reach out to Beth, who would ask Lauren to look at the logs and prepare a report. Lauren's report would usually reveal either a need for more training, a need for more reps, or a good justification for investing in overtime (while reps got up to speed on the new product, for example). Everyone would make an extra effort to learn the new rules or new products and bring his or her call time back down.

But that was before the recent acquisition and the significant growth that followed. Since the merger, all Operations ever did about AHT was send memos to Beth telling her it had to be shorter, but without adding more staff or adding any overtime. It was always "do more with less." In Howard's mind, this wasn't just an empty phrase. He trusted Beth. But he never stopped to consider that as the bank's scope increased, many of its processes weren't as obvious as they once were.

Picking up speed wasn't just a question of getting more serious and working a little harder.

⌐

After the reps had the chance to process their feelings about the frustration they experienced on their shifts, Beth and Lauren stepped them through their new strategy. In a nutshell, until the CRMs were integrated and every rep had access to all the information he needed, any rep who had to step away from his desk for answers to questions that should be in the CRM was eligible for a "pass."

Beth had worked out the "pass" system with Lauren, her chief numbers cruncher, scheduler, and planner. Not every rep would get a pass on AHT, only the ones with a legitimate barrier to completion. If you had more than two calls a day where you had to put the caller on hold while you called another rep because you didn't have access to the answers, you got a pass. If you had not been trained on a new product or a new compliance issue and you received two or more calls about these things, you got a pass. She didn't want it to be seen as an excuse for poor performance. Everything in the call center was measured, and everything would continue to be measured. All Beth was hoping for was to add a little bit of understanding to the mix.

Even before their talks with Beth and Lauren, the call center reps had devised their own work-around: On a whiteboard in every cubicle was either a "GT" for Green Tree or "B" for Bernette, right where other reps could see it to let everyone know which CRM system was at that workstation. That way, all the reps had to do was look down the hallway to know who they had to call for information. Sure, this was a clunky approach.

Any given rep could be on a call at any given time, so there was always waiting involved. But Beth was impressed that the reps had worked out a creative solution themselves, albeit a far from perfect one.

Beth was clear about the temporary nature of the passes. She didn't want anyone to see a pass as an entitlement. It wasn't a permanent fix, and it wasn't necessarily going to make callers any less angry at being on hold for so long. But it would go a long way toward easing the reps' frustration. Now that call center management would offer passes for some instances of low AHT, the reps began to feel that someone was listening to them.

Under the new system, when a rep had to leave her desk to ask another rep for an answer, or when a rep spent time providing an answer to other reps instead of her own callers, a note would be made. After the shift they'd show their notes to their shift supervisor who compiled the "pass time" and gave it to Lauren. Beth would review and approve the passes and Lauren would compensate, adjusting AHT for the affected reps.

From now on, when reps faced "a perfect storm" of obstacles beyond their control that prevented them from performing at their peak, it wouldn't be held against them. When reps' service levels dropped, instead of being penalized, they were invited to explain the situation and to talk about how to improve it.

Even though the new system didn't directly boost service levels, it was a good start. It got everyone on the same page about why service levels fell off from time to time. And it sent a message to the call center representatives: *Management is behind you.* In the meantime, Lauren documented everything she could. She and Beth would have to make a case for expediting the new CRMs, and she needed all the data she could collect.

Little by little over the next few weeks, call center employees began to feel that they had their managers' support. Unfortunately, the excitement was lost on some of the reps who had been experiencing a good deal of frustration over the past months. And it was completely lost on Stacy. Ironically, during her second interview, Stacy and her soon-to-be new boss hit it off while discussing how to enable people to deliver high levels of performance. Of course, that's not what Stacy called it. Nonetheless, she found herself discussing with her new boss how it wasn't enough just to ensure that employees are engaged. "They have to be equipped to do their work," she explained. "That's how I'd make sure that my staff are as engaged on day 100 as they were on day 1."

By coincidence, while Stacy was up late one night preparing for her second interview, Lauren was deleting the cover letter she'd written to a potential new employer. She hadn't sent it yet, but now there was no need. She could feel the changes coming at Bernette, even before they began to happen.

Stacy, on the other hand, was so excited about her new job search that she wasn't paying much attention to Bernette. With one foot out the door, she was looking forward to new challenges and opportunities. She was monitoring a call that had come in to a rep named Katie Lyons, an employee who had been with Bernette for about six months.

Katie, like Stacy, had begun working for Bernette part-time and had moved into a full-time position after only a month. One reason she'd been offered a full-time job was that Stacy liked her attitude. Katie really knew how to handle customers. She was friendly and courteous, and no matter how intense the pressure to complete calls, no caller could have guessed it from her tone of voice. Katie didn't have all the time in the world for your call. But when you were on the phone with her, you'd think she was your private bank representative with no duties other than to help you with your needs. Katie had accepted the offer of full-time employment because she liked working at Bernette; the bank offered good benefits and it had some openings.

But lately, Katie seemed a bit alienated. Lauren had overheard her sounding a little surly on the phone and asked Stacy to keep tabs. Sometimes a rep needed more training, sometimes a little coaching. Bernette had built its reputation on community spirit, good corporate citizenship, and good humor. But Katie didn't seem to realize that—not today, anyway. Stacy slipped her headphones on, punched in the code to monitor Katie, and picked up her current phone call.

The caller explained to Katie that he was brand new to the online experience. The bank executives liked when local customers went online for their banking needs. So much was automated that Bernette was saving a lot of money every year. It hadn't been easy to market online services to its local base of longtime customers. Some didn't trust the Internet, some didn't know how to use it, and others were simply accustomed to doing their banking at a brick-and-mortar bank during business hours. But the marketing group had made some inroads by advertising "the best of both worlds" on local Denver TV stations. Its goal was to persuade existing local customers (like the caller Katie was currently on the line with) that they could have their neighborhood bank with their friendly tellers all day, and an easy-to-use online bank for nights and weekends.

The caller began by stating that he had a couple of reservations about using the Internet to do his banking. He asked how he could be sure that his funds would remain secure and that there would be no risk of identity theft. That was an easy one for Katie. She pulled up the script on her monitor and replied:

"Bernette offers secure sign-in for additional security—"

The customer interrupted. "Secure what?"

"Secure *sign-in*. Like you use for making online purchases from other vendors?"

The caller hesitated for a second. "Sorry, but I've never bought anything online before. This is all new to me."

Katie clicked her tongue impatiently. Stacy heard it. She assumed the caller had as well. "Sir, you did create an online account, right?"

Katie sounded impatient. The way she said "sir" sounded so blunt to Stacy.

Only a month or two earlier, Stacy had been monitoring Katie when she answered the very same questions for another caller. She had spoken the same words she was speaking right now, reading them from her monitor. But something was different. It was her tone of voice.

Stacy continued to monitor as Katie raced through her script to cover encryption and other security features. But she sounded impatient, and Stacy guessed that the customer was feeling it too.

Stacy could feel the frustration in Katie's voice; after all, Katie had to move on to the next call, and this caller—despite his value—was taking up too much of her time. This would reflect poorly in Katie's AHT.

Right then, as if on cue, Stacy's cell phone rang. According to her caller ID, it was Human Resources from the bank across town where she'd had two interviews. She'd been sitting on the offer letter for a couple of days now, and she knew it was time to do something about it. She disconnected from Katie's call, drew a deep breath, and answered brightly, "Hello? Stacy Robbins here."

She'd been correct. It was HR calling about the offer. Everything had been discussed—salary, benefits, the job and all its duties, opportunities for advancement. Now it was time for Stacy to act. Or not.

"Do we have a deal?" asked the HR manager.

Stacy accepted the new position. *Too late for Bernette*, she told herself. She believed that things there could improve. But she also knew she wasn't going to stick around to find out how long it would take. She stayed on the phone with HR for a few minutes, talking about a few perks that were not made clear in the offer letter.

After accepting the offer and hanging up, Stacy sat at her desk, temporarily lost in her thoughts. She recalled an earlier call that Katie Lyons had handled, one that impressed Stacy. The caller was angry, but no matter what he threw at Katie, she remained calm and stayed on point. Mostly what had impressed Stacy (and Beth and Lauren, when she brought it to their attention) was how well Katie connected with the customers, how well she listened, and how clearly and calmly she communicated. At the time, she soothed the caller's anger so effectively that by the end of the call, the customer was actually apologizing and thanking Katie for having hung in there with him!

As if on cue, Katie knocked on Stacy's office door, poked her head in, and asked, "Can we talk?"

That's how Katie Lyons gave her notice. Of course, as a supervisor and a long-term employee, Stacy knew she owed Bernette more than that. After walking Katie to HR for a quick exit interview, Stacy returned to her office, closed the door, sat at her desk, and composed her letter of resignation. She would give it to Lauren before the shift ended. Two weeks should be enough notice, unless they decided to let her go as soon as she tendered her resignation. And actually, she didn't care. She was owed a week of vacation anyway.

The big irony was that Stacy had actually heard about the temporary passes, but she had missed what was most important: Senior management had finally begun to think about the call center reps, what they were up against, why they were frustrated, what the cost to the bank was, and what could be done about it. All she saw were temporary passes. She didn't even want to know what Beth and Lauren were doing to further enable the reps. She couldn't see past her own frustration.

By the end of the first day issuing passes, Beth was exhausted, having spent three days personally meeting with every rep on every shift. But she was exhilarated as well. She could already feel the stirrings of change, and she liked what she felt. She knew if she acted fast she could make a dent in turnover and a big improvement in productivity.

Her phone rang. It was Lauren calling from her office. Beth picked up and immediately began talking about how she could tell the reps were buying in and feeling better already. "Ray is right," Beth told Lauren. "There is a lot we can do on our own right now. I'll talk with Howard and Angela again soon, when we can show them some preliminary numbers. They'll be thrilled!"

There was a slight pause at the other end of the line. "What's the matter?" Beth asked.

Lauren sighed. "Well, there's no easy way to tell you this. Stacy Robbins won't be around for the enablement work. She just turned in her resignation."

Sobering news. Stacy had come to the bank as a teenager and worked herself through college and business school while making her way up through the ranks. She was one of the call center's last links to Bernie Ellsworth and the old Bernette. She was family. And soon she'd be gone.

"I'm so sorry to hear that," said Beth.

"You're not alone," said Lauren.

CHAPTER 10

Diagnosis and Prescription

Now that we have an understanding of the broader issues associated with enabling employees, our focus in this chapter is on helping managers make positive changes to their teams. Like a trip to the doctor, the first step is an examination and diagnosis.

The chapter will lead you through a self-assessment to identify enablement opportunities, encouraging you to look both inward at yourself as a manager and outward at your team's structures and processes. The questions address basic elements of each workplace factor influencing enablement levels, as shown in the Employee Effectiveness Framework presented at the beginning of Chapter 8: Performance Management; Authority & Empowerment; Resources; Training; Collaboration; Work, Structure, & Process. If you find yourself answering "no" to any of these factors, you will have identified a potential focus area. Also included in this chapter are data from Hay Group surveys combined with survey comments from frustrated employees. Our aim is to help you, the manager, diagnose frustration in your team.

Then, with a sense of the highest enablement priorities

within your team, the chapter will help you develop an enablement action plan for your team by exploring the different elements of the enablement factors and their implications.

Performance Management

What Are Frustrated Employees Telling Us?

➤ According to Hay Group surveys, nearly one-third of employees indicate that their managers do not effectively communicate the goals and objectives for their teams.

➤ More than 40 percent report that they do not receive clear and regular feedback from their managers on how well they do their work.

In their own words:

➤ "Communication between managers and employees is very poor. I have not had a performance review in two years, I'm never told expectations for my job, how I'm doing, or how I can improve."

➤ "I have currently been placed in a new role as a result of a reorganization. After five months my manager has yet to provide me with a clear understanding of my roles and responsibilities. I am just 'catching' work that is delegated to me on a day-to-day basis, which causes me concern from a performance management standpoint as well as a career path standpoint. Managers should provide their associates with clear expectations, goals, and objectives so employees have the best chance to succeed and understand their career path."

There are three key considerations to ensuring that performance management enables performance and is not a hindrance or barrier. First, goals and priorities must be clear, to allow individuals to focus their efforts on essential, value-added tasks. Second, goals and priorities must be challenging but attainable, to ensure that they are appropriately energizing and that employees' capabilities are both fully developed and fully used. And third, managers must have regular performance discussions with employees to identify behaviors that may need to be altered and organizational barriers that may be inhibiting individual performance, to ensure that employees are taking the most direct, and efficient, path to goal attainment.

Self-Assessment for Managers: Clarifying Expectations

✓ Do you have a good understanding of your company's performance management process?

✓ Are individual performance goals aligned with organizational priorities and "must-win" battles?

✓ Do you regularly discuss performance expectations with each team member?

✓ Are performance objectives specific and measurable?

✓ When setting performance expectations, do you come to agreement with team members regarding the specific behaviors or activities they should focus on to perform their jobs effectively?

Where it exists, a lack of clarity regarding expectations may have a variety of different causes. In some cases, performance goals may simply not have been established — or defined with sufficient specificity to guide employee efforts. In other cases, communication between managers and employees regarding expectations may be inadequate. That is, managers may have formulated performance goals but failed to communicate them fully to individuals within their teams. In still other cases, managers and their employees may believe that expectations are clear despite a serious lack of alignment. This situation is particularly common where too many goals are put in place for employees to accomplish with a reasonable amount of focus and energy, leading to the likelihood that managers and employees may not see eye to eye on the most critical accountabilities.

It is, therefore, important when managers are clarifying expectations with employees that they create a focused set of specific, measurable goals and clearly lay out the precise behaviors and activities that employees should exhibit to achieve those goals. Likewise, managers need to have sufficient dialogue with each employee to make certain that there is a common understanding of key targets and the tasks most essential to accomplish.

Self-Assessment for Managers: Setting Challenging Goals

▶ Do team members understand what differentiates a high performer from an average performer?

▶ Do you discuss with each employee ways to use his or her core strengths to enhance job performance?

We cannot overstate the importance of setting challenging yet attainable goals. Little else will encourage employees to develop the resourcefulness that discretionary effort requires.

When individuals are faced with challenging goals, they tap into a fuller array of their personal resources and talents in order to achieve these goals. What's more, they demonstrate creativity and resourcefulness as they work to achieve objectives. Challenging goals push individuals beyond their current thresholds of performance.

One way for managers to design challenging yet attainable goals is for them to analyze the achievements of high performers and use such performance as a benchmark. But this shouldn't be done in a vacuum. Rather, goal setting must be accompanied by a discussion with employees regarding how they can bring their specific strengths, skills, and experience to the equation.

Self-Assessment for Managers: Providing Ongoing Feedback

✓ Are formal performance reviews conducted?

✓ Are informal performance discussions held with team members between formal reviews?

✓ Is there currently a process for identifying and addressing poor performance?

✓ Are issues of poor performance addressed in a timely manner?

We, along with many other authors, have discussed the importance of providing ongoing performance feedback to employees. Only with continual feedback can they quickly "course correct" their behaviors back to the most efficient and effective path toward goals and objectives.

However, ongoing performance feedback is rare in most organizations. That's unfortunate, because in general all that's required to make it happen is discipline on the part of managers. Further, and ironically, the more often this type of conversation occurs, the less "uncomfortable" it becomes for both manager and employee. After all, as with most tasks, the more often we undertake them, the easier we find them. And, more important, the more often we have these conversations, the more likely it is that the manager will be required to discuss only modest changes to employee behavior. If a great deal of time passes between feedback conversations, the likelihood is greater that employee behavior will have deviated more substantially from what was expected, leading to a more difficult discussion.

In addition to ensuring a continual process of both formal and informal performance feedback to employees, it is critical that managers consider *how* they will determine that employee performance is veering off course from what is desirable and acceptable. The *how* can range from formal metrics (whether focused on key outcomes or key behaviors) to informal feedback from coworkers. Clearly, managers need to tailor their actions to the specific situation, but the importance of these ongoing conversations is virtually universal.

▷ Deeper Dive: Strategic Performance Management

In conversations with CEOs, we often hear the refrain, "We came up with a good plan and communicated it very clearly, but it is not being carried out. Why?" One reason is poor performance management resulting in poor organizational performance. What is happening at the front line isn't what is necessarily needed to deliver the business results asked for by the CEO. What has been "communicated" has not always been as clearly understood. There is a "disconnect" between strategy and goals at a company level and how these are translated into targets at the team or individual level. Our experience from working with clients to create high-performing organizations reveals the same telltale signs about what is not working. In the majority of cases there is a gap between the work employees do, how their performance is managed, and the impact on achieving business goals.

Performance Management: Hard and Soft

Strategic performance management makes the connection between "hard goals" (business goals and strategy) and "soft goals" (employee motivation and culture). It links an organization's strategy and culture to its managers' ability to improve employees' performance. Most employees want to do the "right" thing, but they can do so only if they know what the right things are and receive regular feedback about their work, if their rewards are aligned, and if they understand the impact they can have on delivering the business strategy. By successfully connecting three things—people, strategy, and culture—CEOs can improve their business results, enhance employee productivity, and increase the likelihood of achieving their business objectives.

What Really Gets in the Way?

Over the years much time and effort has been invested in implementing performance management "best practices" as a way to ensure competitive advantage. Yet for many organizations, these efforts still fail to deliver superior performance. The famous "balanced scorecard" generates a lot of data that managers often have difficulty translating into actions that produce the desired business results. What's more, many managers are concerned about giving feedback that might demoralize hard-working employees or, worse, cause them to leave. Often there is little regular communication between managers and employees—no culture of dialogue. Reward decisions are based on complex processes of translating performance into reward strategies that deliver the wrong results. And despite a big investment in training managers in the processes, procedures, and behaviors needed to implement effective performance management systems, employees complain that their performance systems are too complicated, too technical, and not transparent about how individual performance helps deliver corporate goals.

In other words, strategic performance management is more than just a target-setting process or a way to enhance a leader's ability to give feedback. Rather, it's about aligning company strategy to team and individual goals and rewards, and ensuring that the whole organization is pulling together in the right direction.

Developing a New Performance Model

The missing link is the performance model. It provides guiding principles for the entire set of performance management beliefs, systems, and processes for the business as a whole. A performance model helps to define principles from a strategic and cultural context. By generating transparency across the organization on what the goals are and how they can best be achieved in the current culture, the model creates enormous power and motivation.

To develop a strategic performance model, executives need to ask themselves how they actually want to manage performance in their organization:

- ► What are the key levers in the business model to drive organizational performance?
- ► When looking at strategic targets, what are the key metrics to apply in the measuring systems?
- ► Who is in charge of making it happen?
- ► What is the accountability of line management?
- ► What is the reward philosophy around differentiating performance levels?

> ► How does the organization reward the performance of its best people in terms of career opportunities?
> ► How does management deal with low performance?

Authority & Empowerment

What Are Frustrated Employees Telling Us?

► Fully 30 percent of employees indicate that they do not have enough authority to carry out their jobs effectively.

► Nearly one-third of employees do not feel that their managers encourage them to come up with new and better ways of doing things.

In their own words:

► "I have been given a great deal of responsibility in my present job, but there are too many hurdles to achieving results. Management must empower employees to make decisions by giving them the tools and authority to handle day-to-day operations."

► "I don't think employees are given enough authority in this company. To create an environment that motivates innovation, employees need to feel secure to go outside of the box and be empowered to think responsibly as if they were their own manager/boss."

Appropriate levels of autonomy and empowerment are critical in an enabling environment. Autonomy provides the flexibility employees need to carry out their jobs efficiently and in a way that leverages their skills and abilities. Empowering employees, and encouraging them to come forward with innovative ideas, also allows them to influence the way future work is structured to optimize personal and organizational effectiveness.

> ## Self-Assessment for Managers: Providing Employees with Needed Authority
>
> ✓ Do team members feel empowered to make the decisions necessary to perform their jobs effectively?
>
> ✓ Do employees understand which decisions they control?
>
> ✓ Is there agreement on decision-making accountabilities?
>
> ✓ Are there aspects of the culture, such as fear of consequences, that prohibit employees from making timely decisions?

As we discussed in Chapter 8, authority begins with the clear structuring of decision-making accountabilities. It is critical that employees understand which decisions they can make and which they can't. But even in organizations that have created "specific freedom to act" for employees, high levels of frustration may still be evident. Why? Because while structures may encourage action, negative consequences for decisions out of step with managers' opinions or preferences—or decisions that don't ultimately generate anticipated results—may send the strong signal that playing it safe is the better option. In fact, Hay Group employee opinion norms suggest that more than 40 percent of employees feel that the potential for adverse consequences discourages them from taking actions or making decisions.

Lack of contact with managers may also be a barrier to initiative. With limited interaction, employees may be fearful of getting on a manager's "bad side," since opportunities to correct a negative impression will be few and far between. Managers need to ensure that they are in regular interaction with employees to promote appropriate empowerment and risk taking.

> ### Self-Assessment for Managers: Allowing Employees to Have Input on Work Processes
>
> ✓ Do you intentionally seek information from team members about what is going well and what can be improved in your area?
>
> ✓ Are there formal and informal procedures in place to solicit new ideas both from your team members and from those outside your group?
>
> ✓ Are you creating a climate where team members feel they can share their thoughts and opinions freely?

Managers may perceive themselves to be very open to feedback ("My door is always open"). But the reality, from an employee perspective, may be very different. Therefore, managers need to be conscious about encouraging employees to share perspectives.

Along with soliciting input, managers must be clear on what type of input they want. In many organizations, employees express concerns that input is too often sought *after* decisions have been made. As a result, speaking up may have no impact, and those who do express their opinions risk landing on the wrong side of an issue. Managers need to clarify whether they are asking for employee involvement in *making* a decision or determining how best to *implement* a decision that has already been reached.

Consensus-oriented cultures may also present barriers to speaking up. Where there is a heavy emphasis on driving toward agreement, expressing divergent viewpoints may be seen as confrontational or a signal that an employee is not "with the program" or a team player.

Resources

What Are Frustrated Employees Telling Us?

▶ One-third of employees report that they do not have the resources and information they need to do their jobs well.

▶ More than half of employees express concerns about inadequate staffing levels in their work areas.

In their own words:

▶ "Often we have good ideas, but because we don't have the resources to implement them it discourages innovation and gives employees the impression that we can't change things. This can really create an apathetic work environment."

▶ "Marketing is completely understaffed. Employees leave and there is little urgency to replace them. This leads to low morale, dissatisfaction with pay (because we end up carrying the workload of absent employees), and increased friction between employees. This is the case whether an absence is long-planned or spontaneous."

While the first impulse may be to think of resources as requiring authorizations and allocations from more senior levels in an organization, many of the key resources that impact individual and team enablement are in fact within the control of any manager. People need information, and filling these needs generally requires only the manager's attention and diligence. Physical resources and staff allocations may require budget approvals that extend beyond the manager's direct control. But—as seen in our fictional example of Bernette Financial—managers can play a big role in prioritizing and establishing the ROI of resource requests and in making sure that existing staff resources are managed effectively through efficient planning, scheduling, and training.

Self-Assessment for Managers: Providing Needed Resources

✓ Are there specific resources employees regularly request to help them do their jobs more effectively?

✓ Do you build a business case for resource investments (specifying the anticipated benefits/returns)?

Physical resources require financial commitments from the organization. Consequently, many managers throw up their hands or turn their backs on their responsibility in this area. Yet managers need to acknowledge that while they may lack sole decision-making authority, they are generally the only ones who can advocate on behalf of their employees.

The key here is to *identify* the resources desired, *prioritize* according to the impact on individual and team performance, and then *advocate* based on the returns on resource investments for the organization as a whole. Instead of turning a deaf ear to employee frustrations regarding resources, managers must listen carefully for common themes that can help identify resource barriers to performance and productivity.

Self-Assessment for Managers: Providing Needed Information

✓ Are employees routinely informed when changes are made that affect their work?

> ✓ Do employees hear rumors before you communicate important information?
>
> ✓ Do customers (internal or external) receive information before employees do?
>
> ✓ Do employees have enough information about other groups to interact effectively with them?

In the dynamic environments in which most companies currently operate, employees' thirst for information tends to increase. As a result, managers may struggle to keep up with their demands. Unfortunately, at these times, communication channels in organizations often dry up. Managers, fearful of saying the wrong thing, often say nothing at all. If managers are not providing credible messages, gossip and rumor can be expected to fill the vacuum.

In employee surveys, communication tends to be one of the least favorably rated aspects of organizational performance. And, given the attention many companies devote to getting key messages out, negative ratings in this area often evoke consternation among leaders.

Much of the problem stems from elevated expectations. In a time when information flows ever more freely in many contexts, employees want to be told what they need to know when they need to know it. Give them too much information and they may complain of being overwhelmed with irrelevant or redundant messages. But give them too little and they will express frustration that they are not kept adequately informed about matters that affect them.

Not all managers recognize the role they play as "bridges" or connection points between individuals, work teams, and the broader organization. Managers are the funnels through which information gets to employees. They need to help employees understand what's happening in the organization and what it means for them.

> ### Self-Assessment for Managers: Adequate Staffing
>
> ✓ Do you fill vacancies as quickly as possible?
>
> ✓ Do you manage work schedules to minimize disruptions associated with employee absences?
>
> ✓ Do you analyze staffing needs against forecasted work?

As with physical resources, managers need to assess whether staffing levels are adequate to complete task requirements. If not, staff investments may need to be prioritized. Alternatively, managers may need to consider whether existing staff resources are being used effectively, through appropriate scheduling, filling of vacancies, etc.

It is also important to remember that concerns about staffing may signal problems in other enablement areas. For instance, a manager may have a sufficient number of people but they may be inadequately trained, held back by inefficient processes, unclear on the key things they need to accomplish, or uncertain of their ability to take initiative.

Training

> ### What Are Frustrated Employees Telling Us?
>
> ► More than half of employees report that job demands leave inadequate time to take advantage of job-related training opportunities.

> ► Nearly 50 percent of employees express concerns about the adequacy of training provided to new employees.

In their own words:

> ► "Because it seems that many units are short-staffed, I feel that although training and development is offered, support staff are seldom able to take time off to take advantage of these opportunities. Being absent for an entire day greatly affects the workload in our department, given that backup coverage is seldom available due to the shortage of personnel."

> ► "Employees' best productivity (and good humor!) depends a lot on coworkers knowing the requirements of THEIR jobs. New hires are expected to have a learning period. But training cannot consist of a once-over on rules and requirements. Supervisors need to keep close tabs on what is absorbed and what is forgotten; otherwise, coworkers who have to correct mistakes and fill in for others' lapses quickly become annoyed."

It is important that organizations view training not as an *event* but rather a *process* that unfolds throughout an employee's tenure with the company. Initial training is certainly critical, since in most cases employees do not enter an organization with all the necessary skills and abilities to perform their new roles most effectively. However, to allow employees to improve their performance and enhance their contributions, they must be provided with ongoing opportunities to expand their skill sets.

For employees to be effective in dynamic environments, the training they receive must be continually updated to reflect the new realities they face. Otherwise the skills and abilities that once made an employee a strong contributor can quickly become obsolete.

Self-Assessment for Managers: New Employees

✓ Is there a structured process for initial training of new employees?

✓ Do you set appropriate performance expectations for new employees?

✓ Do experienced employees express frustration over the impact of new employees?

Clearly, the degree to which new employees receive adequate and timely training has a tremendous impact on how quickly they are able to contribute positively to the organization. Yet many organizations provide little (or ineffective) initial training, leading to a much longer than necessary delay in getting new employees up to speed. One common result is frustration among new employees who enter an organization with high levels of motivation and a strong desire to contribute in a significant way, but are unable to have much immediate impact.

Frustrations are likely to be particularly acute if performance goals for new employees are not set at levels appropriate to their skills and abilities. Optimally, performance expectations for new employees should be gradually increased at a rate that is in sync with their expanding capabilities.

The negative consequences of poor initial training extend beyond the frustrations felt by newly hired employees. Indeed, though often unnoticed by managers, the impact may be greatest among longer-tenured employees who are faced with the burden of picking up the slack created by new coworkers who are not able to contribute in meaningful ways. Worse yet, when organizations don't provide adequate formal training to new employees, the task of training these individuals often falls to the longer-tenured employees, which only adds to their existing workload.

Self-Assessment for Managers: Opportunities to Expand Current Skill Sets

✓ Do you have a good understanding of the training and development programs available to employees?

✓ Have you created an inventory of the skills, past work experiences, and educational credentials of your employees?

✓ Have you defined the developmental needs and interests of your employees?

✓ Have you talked with employees about training and development programs, both internal and external?

✓ Are employees discouraged from attending training due to high workload or other organizational barriers?

If organizations are to realize maximum contributions from employees, it is essential to expand their skill sets through ongoing training opportunities. In many cases, employees have untapped capabilities, the capacity to enhance their contributions to the organization with appropriate training. However, managers must be effective at recognizing the potential and interests of each employee, along with the relevant training offerings that exist. Only by understanding both can managers effectively match employees with opportunities.

Though they are often overlooked by managers and organizations, it is critical to understand the barriers that may exist that prevent employees from taking advantage of available training opportunities. Inadequate support for training on the part of managers is an important issue for both individuals and organizations. From the organizational perspective, money spent on developing training programs is wasted if employees have no time to attend.

Over the long term, a continued focus on developing employees is essential. To ensure that adequate numbers of managers and skilled employees are available to fill key roles, organizations need to invest in staff development and avoid the temptation to let short-term demands compromise long-term success.

Self-Assessment for Managers: Skills to Keep Up with Changing Job Demands

✓ Do the requirements and demands of jobs on your team change on an ongoing basis?

✓ Does ongoing training address changing job requirements?

✓ Are accountabilities for identifying shifts in job demands clear?

Most organizations today are in a constant state of change. The big changes are easily recognized and observed. But it is easy for managers to overlook the impact that minor and incremental changes have on the way people do their work. Yet over time, even modest changes can leave an employee's skills and abilities out of sync with the demands of the job, leading to suboptimal performance.

Managers must be sensitive to changing job demands. They must constantly monitor the needs of the workforce from a training and development perspective. In most cases, employees themselves will sense and understand these changes and therefore can be the best sources for managers to understand that training is required. Managers should ensure that defining training needs is a shared accountability between managers and their teams.

Collaboration

What Are Frustrated Employees Telling Us?

▶ Nearly half of employees do not feel that their teams receive high-quality support from other teams within their organizations.

▶ Similar percentages of employees express concerns about the level of encouragement for cooperation and sharing of ideas and resources across the company.

In their own words:

▶ "The workplace and benefits are great here. But there is a problem with departments working as a complete team. We are separated and only concerned about issues that concern our own departments."

▶ "The organization seems to promote the development of little fiefdoms that undermine productivity. As the saying goes, we are only as strong as our weakest link."

A lack of effective collaboration within an organization can be a significant barrier to individuals performing their jobs effectively. The interdependencies that exist between individuals, jobs, and work groups mean that organizations must ensure that all are interacting in a positive and constructive manner, with the understanding that they are working toward a common purpose. Effective collaboration begins with positive teamwork and cooperation within each work unit. From there, it is critical that work units cooperate well with one another, especially when the accomplishment of organizational objectives depends on it. Finally, along with providing support, successful companies understand the need to share resources and information openly and freely across units and functions.

Self-Assessment for Managers: Teamwork Within the Group

✓ Do you assign and coordinate roles well?

✓ Have specific team goals been set and are they clear to all team members?

✓ Does a focus on individual goals interfere with the achievement of team goals?

✓ Is collaborative behavior measured and encouraged by reward and recognition systems?

A lack of intragroup collaboration and cooperation is often the result of a lack of role clarity and accountability. If employees are confused about their individual roles or accountabilities, they will not know on whom they are to depend for help in performing their jobs, nor in what ways others are dependent on them.

It is also critical that managers establish, and make clear to employees, the goals of the group that are shared by all group members. Managers must be sure to identify where individual goals may be competing with shared group goals and work to eliminate, or at least minimize, these obstacles. Further, wherever possible, performance management systems should formally recognize and reward the collaborative behaviors of both individuals and the group as a whole.

Self-Assessment for Managers: Teamwork Across Groups

✓ Are there formal and informal systems in place to promote interdepartmental communication?

✓ Do the objectives of your team/work group/department align with objectives of the teams/work groups/departments you rely on for support?

✓ Does a focus on team goals interfere with the achievement of broader organizational objectives?

✓ Would cross-training between teams/work groups/departments help you better understand how to serve internal customer needs?

✓ Are there reward mechanisms in place to reward and reinforce teamwork and collaboration?

Even in organizations where there are good levels of cooperation and collaboration *within* individual work groups, there may still be a lack of effective teamwork *between* work groups. Again, reward systems might not support the objective of getting everyone to pull on the same end of the rope. Traditionally, businesses overvalue high achievers. Individual accountability is lauded. Companies may claim that the team is paramount and the individual is only a cog in the machine, while they celebrate "Type A" personalities who exceed their targets. This mixes messages; it says that the results of the whole are what matters, then rewards those who maximize the individual parts. If an organization promotes people who have exceeded their targets and run a successful unit while ruining careers and hurting other parts of the business in doing so, the message of collaboration will likely be met with cynicism.

But even if managers and their teams are motivated to collaborate, good intentions may not be enough. In many cases, the root cause of a lack of cooperation is conflict between the operational goals of different departments. More specifically, while everyone may understand how different groups have to rely on one another to be effective, the manner in which they go about their work can create tension that decreases collaboration.

As an example, consider a marketing department focused on innovation and an operations group focused on efficiently answering customer questions. Team members in the two groups may have a collaborative orientation, but different goals (and related practices) may interfere with effective teamwork. The marketing team may be focused on getting products to market quickly, while the operations group proceeds with caution to allow time for testing, troubleshooting, and documentation. In such a case, increased communications between departments can be helpful if it increases awareness of the objectives and needs of each group and if it identifies specific instances of cooperation breakdowns resulting from operational barriers.

Interdepartmental communication may be strengthened by sharing people as well as by sharing information. In many successful companies, moving up means moving around. That is, managers may be placed in a series of roles in different units in different geographies as a way of building a broad perspective on the business. In addition to helping managers think more strategically, a more diverse experience base can also provide knowledge and connections that support collaboration. Likewise, many managers find that establishing some form of cross-training also has a positive impact on cooperation. Again, an understanding of how employees in other groups work makes it easier for employees to develop effective ways to interact and cooperate in pursuit of broader organizational goals.

> ### Self-Assessment for Managers: Sharing Information and Resources
>
> ► Do employees refrain from sharing information for fear of losing control or influence over key processes?
>
> ► Are there formal or informal mechanisms for sharing best practices across teams?
>
> ► Are cross-functional teams used to promote interaction and sharing of information across teams?
>
> ► Are there regular opportunities for employees to interact with people from other teams?

Sharing of information and resources across the organization is critical to achieving optimal levels of performance. Effective knowledge management is, for instance, key to innovation. As noted in Chapter 8, new approaches don't only result from new ideas. "Old" ideas may also serve as the raw material for new ideas, if recombined in productive ways.

However, we often hear managers and employees talk about the many "silos" that exist in their companies. Often the root cause of this state is political. Knowledge is power, and managers and more senior leaders may opt to "protect their turf" instead of sharing information with counterparts in other departments. Unfortunately, this trickles down to employees and impacts their ability to interact effectively with individuals from other groups.

Work, Structure, & Process

> ### What Are Frustrated Employees Telling Us?
>
> ► Nearly half of employees give their organizations low marks for being effectively organized and structured.

> ▶ More than 45 percent of employees report that their or-
> ganizations are insufficiently innovative in using new tech-
> nologies or creative approaches to improve internal
> effectiveness.

In their own words:

> ▶ "As an employee I want to do a good job, but we are
> being held back by the constant work flow changes, many of
> which are not only poorly designed and prematurely imple-
> mented, but result in very poor customer service both exter-
> nally and internally."

> ▶ "Building employees' confidence in their abilities will al-
> low them to be more comfortable in making key decisions. In-
> novations that make our company better should come from
> many directions, not just one (top down)."

As we've seen in the Bernette Financial example, and as we've heard from employees around the world, encouraging hard work and doing more with less will carry an organization only so far and allow it to succeed for only so long. Sustaining high levels of performance requires that employees be able to channel their discretionary efforts productively. Otherwise, over time, motivation will turn into burnout and frustration. Ensuring that work is organized in efficient ways, and backed by efficient processes, is a critical consideration for managers seeking to enable their teams.

Self-Assessment for Managers: Structuring Work Processes for Efficiency

✓ Are there well-defined procedures for performing the work?

✓ Do employees know and understand work procedures?

✓ Are work procedures modified when objectives and requirements change?

Structure and processes are keys to facilitating efficient execution of objectives and coordinating the efforts of individuals and teams by promoting consistent expectations and clarifying roles and responsibilities. In other words, they reflect established routines for accomplishing regular tasks in regular ways. But along with the benefits they bring to organizations comes a potential trap: Where requirements change, perhaps due to shifts in the business environment, existing ways of working may no longer work. Therefore, managers need to define work procedures and communicate them clearly to employees, but they also need to evaluate processes regularly to ensure that roles and work systems are aligned with present work demands.

Self-Assessment for Managers: Coordination with Other Units

✓ Do reporting relationships and formal structures interfere with operating effectively with other groups?

✓ Are the accountabilities of different groups clear so that employees know who is responsible for what?

✓ Have shared goals been defined across units?

Jobs and processes should be designed to support collaboration and coordination among individuals, teams, functions, and business units. Interdependencies need to be crystal clear across the organization to avoid redundancies or gaps in accountabilities between jobs or roles in organizational processes. Employees need to know who is responsible for what to avoid working at cross-purposes or duplicating efforts. Given the rapid pace of change in many of today's organizations, it is easy for "handoffs" to become unclear, leading to inefficiencies or reluctance to act.

Likewise, given the "white space" between business units and functions that many organizations have created through flatter structures, broader roles, and the use of teams, decision making has become more complex. Where managers or employees share accountabilities or resources, the interdependencies need to be explicit, with clear procedures in place to resolve disputes or uncertainties quickly and decisively.

Self-Assessment for Managers: Leveraging New Technologies/Approaches

✓ Does your team have a culture of continuous improvement?

✓ Are you proactive in identifying improvement opportunities (fixing things before they are broken)?

✓ Do you identify clear priorities for innovation and improvement?

✓ Are you sufficiently patient with new ideas that don't pay off immediately?

✓ Are there mechanisms in place for bringing new ideas and thinking into your group (outside experts, consultants, customers, new hires)?

In our view, "innovation" is an organizational capability rather than something that springs from "Eureka moments" of individuals or exclusively from selected functions such as R&D. All managers therefore have a role to play in facilitating innovations to improve how their teams do their work.

Innovation offers potential benefits for companies, but it

also presents real costs in terms of both money and time. To maximize the return on investments, managers need to focus efforts by clearly defining the areas in which new ideas and approaches are to be pursued.

Our research with the World's Most Admired companies indicates that they manage implementation by ensuring that change occurs at an adequate but realistic pace. They avoid the temptation to take on all opportunities and challenges at once. Being selective about initiatives pursued promotes a higher ROI.

Managing the pace of change also means balancing patience and accountability. Innovative companies ensure that individuals and groups initiating new approaches see them through to full implementation. But they are also more likely than other companies to report that they resist the temptation to "pull the plug" too quickly on promising ideas that don't generate immediate returns. We find that the most successful companies in this area take an active approach to promoting and managing innovation. To maintain differentiation through innovation, they foster a culture of improvement and continually seek to reinvent themselves. They do a better job than other companies of proactively addressing potential problems before they occur. In these companies, managers and employees are also more likely to be encouraged to innovate in areas of current strength. In other words, they have license to "fix" things that aren't broken.

We can gain further insight into management's role in fostering innovation by drawing on Hay Group's normative databases on leadership styles. Hay Group's Inventory of Leadership Styles is designed to provide managers with feedback from their direct reports on their dominant leadership styles. Our databases include data from some of the world's most innovative companies, collected over decades. The data, compiled from actual feedback provided by managers' subordinates, suggest that leaders in the most innovative companies exhibit a distinctive profile. Prevalent leadership styles include:

- ▶ *Authoritative* (providing strong vision and direction)
- ▶ *Affiliative* (fostering harmony within the team)
- ▶ *Participative* (building commitment and generating new ideas)
- ▶ *Coaching* (focusing on long-term individual development)

Managers with high-performing teams commonly demonstrate these leadership styles. What's more, these leadership styles are conducive to innovation and foster high levels of direction, empowerment, participation, and teamwork.

⌐

The self-assessment in this chapter was intended to help you think more deeply about enablement factors within your team and begin to identify opportunities to enhance the ability of your people to deliver their best efforts. Along the way, hopefully the exercise has reinforced that there is much that individual managers can do on their own to both diagnose and address potential sources of employee frustration.

While you don't need to wait for approval or support from more senior leaders to begin making positive changes, it is of course likewise true that no team within an organization is an island. Your success in enabling your people will be influenced by broader organizational dynamics. In the subsequent chapters we will discuss the role managers can play as change agents, helping to elevate awareness of enablement issues within their organizations and advocate for improvements in systems and processes that extend beyond their immediate spheres of influence.

CHAPTER 11

Starting to Get Results

BERNETTE'S ENABLEMENT WORK was off to a good start. Now that Beth was attending the monthly marketing meetings, the call center had greater access to information about new products in development and their anticipated launch dates. Call center AHT dropped and—according to the latest surveys—customer satisfaction was up as well.

With the new emphasis on clear communications with marketing about new products, not only did the call center's service levels begin to improve, but the reps also began to up-sell bank products to callers. Howard noticed an immediate uptick in sales, the first measurable indication that enablement would lead to bigger revenues.

Getting an invitation to the marketing meeting was easy. All Beth had to do was ask her peers in the marketing department. But the legal department was harder to crack. Beth went to Howard for support, and he asked the legal team to involve Beth in all compliance decisions that could affect customer service. Within a week, she had a standing invitation to the legal department's quarterly compliance review, where tax changes and relevant legislation were discussed.

"No one likes surprises," Beth explained to Howard. "At least not the kind of surprises that slow down our work. From now on," she explained, "when a legal compliance issue arises that will require additional training for the call center team, we'll be involved in making decisions about when to schedule the training. That way, we can be sure that we'll be able to keep the call center fully staffed without having to make use of overtime that is often unwanted and always expensive."

"Such a simple solution," he said to Beth. "Why didn't I think about this before?"

Beth smiled. "Don't beat yourself up. Ray Pough told me he never thought about it either until he left Bernette. Sometimes having a little distance can really open your eyes."

"Thanks for your persistence," said Howard. "And when you talk with Ray, thank him too, and ask him to give me a call."

Lauren found it easy to measure time spent tracking down answers that were not in a rep's CRM and making the appropriate adjustment. The passes allowed several extra minutes to get tacked on to a rep's AHT (under certain circumstances). Lauren didn't see anyone trying to take advantage of the system. Some reps didn't need passes because while they had only Green Tree CRMs they responded only to Green Tree customers. But any rep who had to navigate hallways and other people's cubicles in search of information got a pass.

Since the initial communication plan had worked out so well, there were no misunderstandings, no complaints about one rep getting away with shorter AHT than others. "It's like a golf handicap," observed one rep named Rachel. "It really does make things more like apples to apples."

Those were the sentiments expressed time and time again by the reps who only weeks earlier had felt harried. A few had been on the verge of quitting, but not anymore.

Interestingly, no one tried to make Bernette a more fun place to work or attempted to improve morale. Based on their in-depth discussions leading up to the new strategy, middle managers and senior managers agreed that that would likely improve when the frustration was alleviated. And the frustration wasn't going to be alleviated until the call center representatives were enabled.

While the new pass strategy had been implemented with relative ease, Beth hoped that the results would encourage Howard and Angela to push CRM integration up. Now that Beth could show them what the lack of integration was costing the bank, she was confident that they'd reevaluate their priorities. Within a few weeks, integration could happen, the reps would get the CRM training they needed, and before long the passes would be a thing of the past. "Get enabled and stay enabled," Beth commented to Lauren one day. "It's a never-ending process because there are always new things to learn. But now that I've seen the numbers and spoken with the reps, I can see there is no other sensible way to do it. And I'm convinced that when we make our next presentation to Howard and Angela, they'll agree."

Since Stacy hadn't been replaced yet, Lauren was taking on some extra supervisory duties such as monitoring calls. One morning she was delighted to listen in on a call that was being handled by a rep named Peter, who only a month earlier had been put on an action plan. Today there was something in Peter's voice and his attitude with the caller that signaled positive changes to Lauren. Peter had previously been warned about being short-tempered and impatient with callers. Yet today he was showing a new side of himself. Lauren was impressed. After the call ended, she called Peter back and invited him to stop by her office. When he arrived a few minutes later, she complimented him on his new and improved attitude.

Peter shrugged and thanked her. "I didn't actually do anything to change," he explained. "I just feel like Bernette has become a much better place to work lately. I know how hard you and Beth worked to implement the pass system. Even on days when I don't need a pass, just the fact that I have some breathing room makes all the difference in the world. And it's not just me, you know."

Lauren was happy to hear this. Peter hadn't received much direction after his last performance review. He'd been warned that if he didn't improve his attitude he could lose his job. But that hadn't changed him. The action plan was implemented, and neither Beth nor Lauren had held out much hope. But now, suddenly, he seemed to have made a big adjustment on his own. "Keep up the good work," Lauren told him as he headed back to his desk. She printed out a transcript of the call she had just monitored. While it had taken nearly three minutes longer to complete than it should have, Peter had a pass because he had missed critical training and had to put the customer on hold while he researched her question. Yet when he got back on the phone, he was so pleasant and so eager to help that the customer didn't mind being kept waiting. She even thanked him for taking his time to find out what she needed. "Feel free to call back any time you need assistance," he reminded the customer at the end of the call. "And you can also find answers to your questions in our new and improved customer service website."

As she reviewed the transcript, Lauren was amazed by what a little enablement could do. Peter wasn't naturally surly and impatient. Once the source of frustration was eliminated, his attitude changed. Beth reminded herself: *That is why we hired him in the first place. We're good at screening for the type of personality that's a good fit here. If that were Peter's true nature, we never would have hired him.*

Frustration. That was the culprit. And the good news was that it would be easier to enable frustrated people than to engage demotivated ones. Enablement was about giving people the tools they needed, the resources, the training, and the appropriate job alignment—just what the call center employees were asking for! That seemed more practical than figuring out how to fire up people who weren't engaged.

"After listening to what the reps have to say," Beth told Lauren one night when they went out together after work, "I realized that their concerns really resonate with the things about this job that keep me up at night."

Lauren had worked with Beth for so long, she knew what concerned her boss without even having to ask. "Right," she said. "It's the same thing that keeps me up at night. Can our employees deliver on our customer service promise?"

Beth smiled. "Exactly," she said. "And now I'm finding it exciting that we're drilling down—as an organization, not just as a department—and tying that customer service promise to the bank's mission."

This was more than just talk. If the customer service promise wasn't real, if it wasn't tied to the bank's mission, call center reps would know, and so would customers. When the mission is part of the customer service promise, Beth reasoned, some calls might take longer than were previously allowed. But in theory, reps would pour their discretionary effort into their jobs. "Once we enable them to perform at their peak, I believe they will perform at their peak. And if we measure all that extra effort against what it costs in AHT, we are going to come out ahead."

Lauren agreed. "It's interesting that we work in a call center, where everything gets measured. If other departments felt the drag of a lack of enablement, their managers would be able to identify it. But they might not have the tools to measure it like we do. In a couple months, I'll have a report that shows how enabling our employees goes directly to the bottom line."

Of course, both women knew that this kind of success wouldn't happen in a vacuum. They still needed to hire the right people. And they had to look carefully at training and at their own management development systems to make sure that enablement would become part of the culture. "Enablement is like engagement's twin," said Beth. "Put them together and they'll work in tandem to put out more effort. But keep them apart and the people who are engaged will become frustrated."

"Right," said Lauren. "In fact, those engaged people might just be the first to feel the frustration, because they are the ones who most want to succeed."

Before scheduling a presentation to the senior executives, Beth and Lauren reached out to Ray Pough again. Ray agreed to meet the women at "the usual place"—the coffee shop near the bank.

Over coffee one morning before work, Beth and Lauren filled Ray in on the enablement work to date and the gains they'd been seeing. Ray was pleased to hear the good news.

"But we know that there are some things we can't fix on our own," said Beth. "If we could get senior leaders involved, we could do even more."

Ray sipped his coffee and thought for a moment. "When you approach Howard, try to see yourselves as the voice of Bernette's frustrated employees," he said. "Tell him why these voices are often unheard and why senior leaders like him are often unaware of enablement issues. In some organizations, senior management just isn't asking. In others, senior management is asking, but they can't really hear the answer. And in still others, senior management just doesn't want to know."

Lauren agreed. "I think with us, senior management just wasn't asking."

"You're on the right track," said Ray. "It's about building awareness of the issues as well as a business case for addressing them."

The next day at a call center department meeting, enthusiasm was in the air. "I am so happy that we're doing this," said Rachel, the rep who had mentioned her rising AHT to Lauren just a few weeks earlier. Beth could see the relief in Rachel's face—and hear it in her voice—when she spoke up at the meeting during her shift. "It was so frustrating, I admit I was starting to look for another job." Several of her colleagues nodded in agreement. "It seemed like every time I mentioned anything about it, all I got was—"

"Do more with less!" several of the reps called out wryly.

Lauren chuckled. "I like our new approach better."

After everyone shared a laugh, they got back to business. "My AHT was pretty good a year and a half ago," said Rachel.

"I used to watch it because I'm a naturally competitive person. I've always wanted to be the best. But at some point after the merger, when my AHT started to go up even after I got up to speed on a new product, I began to wonder if monitoring my own call times and trying to improve myself was even worth the effort." Rachel described how she sometimes took it upon herself to make informal follow-up calls to make sure her customers had been able to resolve their issues. "But eventually, I lost interest in that because no matter what I did, it didn't seem to matter. I'm pretty good at this. I'm diligent, and my biggest competitor is myself. I never fell too far behind. But I did fall. And when I realized I was up against a wall, I admit that I did stop trying so hard."

Rachel had been one of the reps who devised the system for knowing who was on the phone and who wasn't, and who had which bank's CRM. That work-around saved a few minutes a day, but it wasn't sophisticated enough to alleviate either the callers' or the call center representatives' mounting sense of frustration. "It was taking me three minutes to do what I was supposed to do in two minutes. And because most of that time was spent walking to and from other people's cubes in search of answers that were supposed to be at my station, what was I going to do? If I'd run up and down the hallways, then I'd be out of breath by the time I got back on the phone. And that wouldn't come off as very professional. So I did my best. But when I learned that my best wasn't good enough, to be perfectly honest, part of me just gave up."

Other reps in the group voiced their agreement. There was some general discussion of "call center math" and the difference between doing more with less and doing the impossible. "What you guys were asking us to do was impossible," Rachel said.

Other reps talked about their own frustration. Once they started talking, one story led to another, and nearly all the stories arrived at the same conclusion: When you are asked to do the impossible, you won't work any harder. In fact, you probably won't work as hard. Why should you if you're destined to fail?

After that meeting, Beth and Lauren decided the time was right to present everything they had on enablement to senior management. Before they scheduled the meeting, they made sure they had good data to present and a sound argument for installing new CRM tools. They felt they had done most of what they could accomplish on their own without getting the senior team involved. The passes had enabled employees; the improvements in communication were getting good results. But they couldn't do anything about the CRM situation on their own.

Before meeting with Howard and his team, Beth decided to talk again with a number of customer service reps to get more feedback about what was frustrating them and what they believed would enable them.

Once people began opening up, Beth learned more about their concerns. Her earlier conclusion was confirmed. She and Lauren were hiring good people who had the right characteristics to work in call centers: good voices (for the phone) or good writing skills (for e-mail), patience, and strong interpersonal skills. She didn't plan to change her hiring practices. She'd always had good instincts. After all, she'd hired Lauren as well as a number of the bank's top call center reps. She believed that people there were engaged in their work. They cared. When she asked them about the bank's mission, most of them knew what it was. The bank was there to serve the community, but that was easy to lose sight of with so much emphasis on AHT and on service levels.

Was the mission relevant to call center employees, or had it become just a talking point?

Discussing this with the reps, Beth came to understand that they just weren't seeing how they were supposed to buy in to that mission. One rep smiled sarcastically when Beth asked her about it. "We're here to help families buy homes and blah, blah, blah," she said. "See? I know what our mission is."

Beth had promised herself not to judge anything she heard employees say during these talks. She wanted to understand how people were feeling. Letting them talk, not arguing with them or shutting them down, was the way to do that.

"You sound a bit cynical about the mission," Beth told the rep. "Can you talk to me about that?"

"Sure," said the rep. "I mean, I know that is supposed to be our mission. But, honestly, when was the last time any supervisor talked about the mission to one of us reps during our reviews?"

Beth raised her eyebrows, not in defiance but with surprise. The rep was right. Under the "less is more" banner Beth couldn't recall the last time the bank's mission came up at a performance review.

The rep continued. "As long as you're asking, I'll be honest. I've been working here for seven months. I just had my six-month review with Stacy, who is no longer with the organization. And don't get me wrong: I adored Stacy. But let's get real. We talked about how to improve my AHT. We talked about how I could handle more calls in less time and avoid escalation. But helping people? Sorry, that never actually came up. So, really, what does the mission have to do with what I do here every day?"

Beth resolved to address the issue. At every review, she told herself, the manager conducting it would talk about the bank's mission as well as how the employee's performance tied into it. Yes, they would still talk about AHT and service levels, but they would talk about the mission as well. They would talk about how it aligned (or didn't align) with the employee's job. Tracking people's "numbers" wasn't going away, but people's numbers had to be considered in the context of the bank's strategy. No longer would it be solely about how long each call took, how many were resolved, and how many were escalated.

⌐

As Beth and Lauren exited Howard's office, they congratulated each other. Their presentation had gone well. After hearing Beth's business case, the senior executive team decided to push CRM integration to the top of Bernette's priorities. "I can't tell you how much I appreciate you bringing this issue to me," Howard told the two women at the end of the meeting. "Your presentation helped us all understand what the CRM problem is costing us." He acknowledged that while Beth and Lauren had made some good steps to address employee frustration, "there are times when it's necessary to approach things from an organizational perspective." And he told Beth he wanted her to "have a seat at the table" for senior management's weekly department heads meeting.

That night when she got home from work, Lauren was so relieved by the new developments that she called her father to tell him. Phil could hear it in her voice. "It's visceral, isn't it?" he asked.

"That's a good way to put it," she told him. "I can feel the change in my gut!"

It wasn't until that moment that Lauren realized how stressed out she had become about work. This was uncharacteristic of her.

She was generally easygoing. It wasn't until that moment, on the phone with her father, that it occurred to her that for the past few months, whenever she was not at work but thought about work, she felt a nagging sense of dissatisfaction. "If I hadn't believed so much in the bank," she told her father on the phone, "I think it would have been easier for me just to let go and find a new job or, worse, just to stick it out there and not really have my head in the game."

"Right," said her father. "Back in the day, my best designers were the ones who not only believed in the product we were developing, but had the resources they needed to build it. When designers met with resistance from management, or they didn't have access to the information they needed to do good R&D, I could just see them sort of shut down. And these were trained professionals, so I can only imagine how much faster a frustrated call center employee shuts down."

He told her how his teams had always burned the midnight oil, even when they didn't have to. "Even when we weren't on deadline," he explained, "these guys were so driven, they'd be at the office late every night. Now there's nothing wrong with leaving the office at 5:30 after a full day's work, but in my profession I always preferred to rely on my people giving a little something extra. And you know what? At the end of the day, that little something extra made the difference between getting our prototypes out on time and ultimately beating our competitors to market."

"I hear you," said Lauren. "It's the same at the call center. When we can get our reps to give that little bit extra I know we're outclassing our competition." Of course, the reps were hourly employees, so it wasn't about working more hours. It was about getting more done in the hours they were there.

In Lauren's environment, the extra effort had to do with commitment to the customer, with going the extra mile for the person on the phone. It was about being aware of how long the call was taking, but at the same time never letting the caller hear the rep's impatience. "And for us, it's about turnover too," she said. "If my people are frustrated, Bernette becomes a revolving door."

"Ironic," said Phil, "that under the right circumstances, you get your people to work harder for you, they have a better time doing it, so they thank you by working even harder."

After she got off the phone with her father, Lauren breathed a sigh of relief. Finally, she thought. She and her manager had persuaded the decision makers that there was a problem that needed to be addressed. It had been there for all to see. But sometimes, she realized, you need an outside eye—like Ray Pough—to recognize the patterns and recommend a practical solution.

~~

While some results would not be seen for months, one almost immediate benefit of the changes was Bob the writer's promotion to marketing. In his new role, Bob quickly became a shining light. He began by revising the customer service section of Bernette's website. With measuring improvements in mind, Bob asked one of his new colleagues for a baseline on customer calls. "I can't know how much better the new customer service section is working until I know how well it worked before," he explained to one of the "data architects" assigned to the new project.

Bob was confident that a new customer service section would reduce the number of calls to the call center and improve business. "It's a win-win," Bob told Lauren on his last day in the call center. "I know Bernette's policies like the back of my hand." There was another aspect to Bob's success: Reps felt empowered. They got a message, loud and clear, that the senior team had handed more decision-making authority to the call center managers. And that authority would be put to good use.

CHAPTER 12

Managers as Agents of Organizational Change

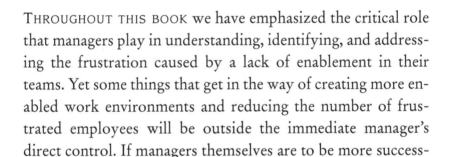

THROUGHOUT THIS BOOK we have emphasized the critical role that managers play in understanding, identifying, and addressing the frustration caused by a lack of enablement in their teams. Yet some things that get in the way of creating more enabled work environments and reducing the number of frustrated employees will be outside the immediate manager's direct control. If managers themselves are to be more successful by helping their direct reports achieve success, they may need to look beyond their teams.

Consider our fictional example, the call center at Bernette Financial. The call center's managers saw the problems created when communications about new products and new regulations that affected call center operations, scheduling, and training were inadequate. Unable to change the trickle-down of messages on their own by building structure around the bank's communication policies, the call center managers appealed to the bank's executives, making a sound business case for a change in how information about new bank products and legislation relevant to the call center was shared.

The managers' business case was a graphic demonstration of how a lack of timely communications cost the bank money through increased turnover, decreased customer satisfaction, and overtime pay. Ultimately, the call center managers persuaded the senior team to make some adjustments that enabled the frustrated customer service representatives, improving customer satisfaction at the same time.

Sometimes enablement requires communication and collaboration horizontally as well as vertically. At Bernette, the genesis of Bob the writer's move from customer service to marketing was a discussion between his immediate manager and her peer in the marketing department. But the decision required approval from more senior leaders. Bob's manager and her marketing colleague could only identify the problem and recommend a solution. But they were not authorized to change the bank's work processes. That required an appeal to senior management. They made their appeal by making a strong business case. They didn't simply argue that Bob would be happier in marketing. They showed how much it cost to keep Bob in customer service as well as how cost-effective it would be to transfer him to marketing.

Whether working horizontally or vertically, managers can play an important role as "organizational change agents." Like the call center managers at Bernette, they can build awareness by helping leaders understand, as you now do, that frustration exists in the organization, that it creates a demotivating environment, and that the root cause is a lack of enablement. Most call center representatives at Bernette wanted to do an outstanding job. But they were frustrated by the bank's performance management system; authority and empowerment issues; a lack of resources; training that arrived too late; an atmosphere where collaboration had suffered as the bank grew; and work, structure, and process issues. Some systems and processes had outgrown the informal structures that existed. Communications used to trickle down from senior management to the call center, but the cascade of messages broke down in a larger organization. Adding some structure enabled call center employees to perform at a higher level.

Managers who understand the causes and implications of employee frustration can build the business case to motivate leaders to enable employees. At Bernette, Beth and Lauren were not authorized to purchase new CRM tools, nor were they allowed to decide when the tools would be implemented. While they could devise work-arounds that aided the customer service representatives and helped improve the situation to a degree, they would never have resolved the issues without broad organizational support. But they didn't just sit around and wait for that support. They made a business case that won senior management buy-in. The business case they made helped the entire department get traction, and it gave them credibility across the senior team.

Overcoming Barriers to Enablement

Being an organizational change agent means giving voice to the frustrated employee, just as Beth and Lauren did at Bernette. We have discussed reasons why enablement issues are often overlooked in organizations. It's up to the manager who understands frustration to help overcome these barriers, which include:

▶ *Failure to ask.* The organization may not have systems in place to hear employee frustration, such as a regular employee survey that focuses on both engagement and enablement issues.

But don't forget, managers have the ability to ask employees directly. Managers who understand that frustration is a major cause of performance problems need to discuss sources of frustration directly with employees. They can start by asking members of their teams, "What are the barriers to your doing your job well? How can the conditions of your job change to help you do it better?" One natural context in which to ask these questions is the ongoing dialogue around performance that managers generally recognize should happen but often doesn't. This doesn't involve some new initiative but rather something core to the manager's role.

▶ *Inability to hear.* Asking employees directly about their frustration also helps get around the "we can't hear them" problem. As we noted earlier, motivated and engaged employees are often disinclined to voice their concerns. They may believe that things are unlikely to change and that voicing their concerns will have no impact or, worse, will make them look like complainers. High-achieving employees want to be seen as loyal and committed to helping the organization succeed. They may feel that by pointing out the things that the organization could do better, they will be seen as pessimistic rather than "good" employees who are devoted to helping the company. Most employees don't want to be seen as causing problems for their managers; good employees make life easier for their bosses, not harder by complaining. Therefore, by being proactive in these discussions, managers can create a "safe zone" for employees to voice their specific reasons for frustration. By asking, "How can we change things around here to help you be more effective?" a manager creates an opportunity for an employee to speak honestly and openly about enablement issues.

If you don't ask, employees may feel that the right thing to do is to say nothing. But if you pose the question, then the positive and helpful thing to do is to give a response. Simply by asking, you flip the situation 180 degrees!

► *Reluctance to know.* Sometimes we avoid dealing with frustration because it's a lot easier to see the costs of addressing enablement issues than it is to see the ultimate savings or benefits. By understanding the root causes and the negative impact of workplace frustration—whether directly (through increased costs or decreased revenue) or indirectly (through "soft" costs such as turnover, or opportunity costs such as a lack of motivation to exceed job expectations)—individual managers can help senior leaders see the business reasons for making changes. There may be a general awareness in the organization that some things are amiss in terms of enabling conditions, but given other "urgent" priorities action isn't taken. However, like we saw at Bernette, if managers can confront leaders with real-time information, feedback, and data, they can promote a focus on key enablement issues. What is said will probably not come as entirely surprising news, but leaders may not be fully aware of its importance or its implications.

"Doing More with Less"

We heard a lot about "doing more with less" at Bernette Financial. And the expression has become something of a battle cry for many of today's organizations. But what exactly does "doing more with less" mean?

There's a facile answer: For many companies, it means continually raising the bar on goals and expectations for individuals and departments across the organization, while at the same time spending less money. That is, it typically involves trying to motivate employees to work harder. And for employees, it means that management is going to want you to work more hours or accomplish more in the same amount of time. And because management is watching costs, you will likely not be given what you need to do the job well. It's frustrating, especially to employees who are engaged, loyal to the organization, and want to achieve excellent results.

Consequently, these employees respond by hunkering down and soldiering on, despite feeling overworked and overburdened.

At Bernette, "do more with less" was a message that eventually demotivated employees, increased turnover, and decreased customer satisfaction. Certainly, the bank's call center had a good number of committed and loyal employees who devised shortcuts and work-arounds in an effort to accomplish more per shift. But they couldn't maintain service levels on their own. As Stacy pointed out to her supervisor, if you're building a house and your crew is short one person for a day or two, perhaps everyone else can pitch in, arrive on site a little earlier, stay a little longer, pick up some of the slack, and accomplish the same amount of work that they would have if they weren't one person short. Or say the crew is missing one hammer. That won't stop them from building the house. It may take a little bit longer if two people have to share the same tool. But it won't crush the project. However, if one or more crew members leave for good, or all the tools are missing, the house won't get built. You can tell a crew with no tools to do more with less, but those are just empty words. They'll only demotivate.

Bottom line: In any business, demanding more and more

effort from employees may produce positive results in the short term, but it is not sustainable in the long term.

Yet, armed with an enablement perspective, "doing more with less" has a different implication. The traditional view, from both the organization and employee perspective, is all about what *employees* need to do to help organizations accomplish more with fewer resources. But the enablement view shifts the focus to how *managers and leaders* need to respond. In this context, "doing more with less" doesn't mean conjuring higher levels of motivation out of thin air, but rather allowing motivated employees to perform at their best. It's about harnessing and unleashing the full potential of frustrated employees — those who want to give their best but can't due to organizational barriers and constraints. Organizations can do more with less simply by not leaving so much untapped performance on the table.

We don't mean to suggest that enabling employees involves providing them with everything they might want. Of course, organizations face resource constraints. Instead, leaders and managers need to have an understanding of the critical enablement drivers of performance and focus their limited resources in those areas.

Instead of concentrating exclusively on fostering higher levels of motivation, managers and leaders need to take better advantage of the motivation they already have. In our work with many of the world's leading organizations, we have found that the remedy for frustration is enablement. Enabled employees will work harder and produce more because that's what they've wanted to do all along.

Epilogue

THIS YEAR'S HOLIDAY PARTY at Bernette Financial was, by all accounts, the best ever. Because of a dip in the economy, the budget for the party wasn't as big as in previous years. Instead of the usual jazz quartet, there was a DJ. Instead of being held at one of Denver's luxury hotels, it took place in the banquet hall of a popular restaurant. But none of that mattered to the employees and their families, or to the handful of board members, select customers, and friends of the bank who attended. Everyone ate, drank, chatted, and danced. The banquet hall was abuzz!

There was much to celebrate, even in a recession. For starters, after Thanksgiving the bank's board of directors had approved the long-awaited reorganization. Finally, Bernie could retire and Howard could take over as CEO. The bank would remain a privately held institution. Bernie—the bank's founder and visionary—had hoped for this outcome.

Executives, middle managers, and rank-and-file employees were happy to know that Howard would soon be installed as CEO. Bittersweet as it was to bid farewell to Bernie, everyone was excited about what was happening at the bank, its growth as well as its direction. Two weeks ago, *Denver Magazine* had again named Bernette one of the city's top ten places to work.

Away from the crowd, far from the music, Beth Charles and Ray Pough sat at a small table, chatting about their children, their upcoming ski vacations, and whether the Broncos had a shot at the Super Bowl. After a while, the conversation turned back to where it had begun: Bernette Financial.

Ray sipped his punch, looked around the crowded banquet hall, and said, "This is a holiday party after all, so I'm not surprised that everyone looks so happy. But I have to think some of Bernette's good cheer these days comes from the enablement work that you and Lauren did this year."

Beth raised her glass and toasted Ray. "We couldn't have done it alone," she said. "Your advice and your insights were golden. I can't thank you enough, Ray."

In response, Ray smiled mysteriously. Beth eyed him with curiosity.

"Wait a second," she said. "What's that look you're giving me?"

"Nothing," Ray protested. "I'm just enjoying the atmosphere. I was talking to Bernie earlier. He told me that he is going out exactly the way he wanted to, with the bank doing well and his son taking over the reins."

"Bernie is great," said Beth. "And obviously, the enablement work would have gone nowhere if it weren't for him and his team. Once they understood why my people were frustrated, they weren't afraid to make the necessary changes."

Indeed, the new CRM system ushered in a new level of service and new heights in customer satisfaction. But that wasn't all. Now that Beth had "a seat at the table" and attended executive management meetings, she knew about the legislative changes, tax issues, and new products that were relevant to the bank's customers. That was one of the easier adjustments, more attitudinal than operational. The others—performance management, especially—took more time and more commitment from Howard and his team. But the commitment was there, driven by the understanding that a lack of enablement frustrates employees, inhibiting their opportunities to shine.

Since a lot of what happens in a customer service department gets measured, it was relatively easy to see the connection in that department between management's enabling employees and the bank's reaping positive business results. Service levels improved, customer satisfaction surveys went up, and overtime pay went down. Not every department measures satisfaction or pays overtime the way customer service does. Nonetheless, every department in the bank experienced lower turnover, which went directly to Bernette's bottom line.

Beth tried one more time. "Ray, I feel like you've been holding something back. Every time someone asks you what you've been doing since you resigned from Bernette, you hem and haw and don't give a straight answer. Is something wrong? I'm your friend, Ray. You can talk to me if—"

Ray cut in. "That's kind of you, Beth. I appreciate your concern. It's true: I *have* been cagey about what I've been doing since I left Bernette, but I'm ready to come clean. Over the past year I've been working on a special project, something I've had in mind for a long time. . . ."

Now Beth's curiosity was even more aroused. "Tell me," she said. "I'll keep it under my hat if you want."

"Well," Ray began, clearing his throat and setting his glass on the table. "In fact, I've been writing a book."

"Really," said Beth. "What's it about?"

"It's about everything we've been discussing," said Ray. "It's about how to enable frustrated employees."

Beth was impressed and surprised. "That's fantastic!" she said.

"I'm glad you feel that way," said Ray. He took another long sip of punch, the mischievous smile still on his face.

"I can't wait to read it," said Beth. "But I can tell from the look on your face that there's more to the story. So spill it!"

"Okay, I will," he said. He raised his hands in reassurance. "Now, don't worry, I changed everyone's name, and the city, and the name of the bank. But you and Lauren, Stacy, Angela, and Howard and Bernie, Bob the writer—you're all in it."

"That's terrific," Beth replied. "We have a great story, and I look forward to seeing it in print. But when will the book be done?"

"Actually," Ray said with a grin, "I just finished it. Right now."

Index